Exercises for
Understanding
English Grammar

SAVE
ON
USED
BOOKS

Exercises for
Understanding
English Grammar

EIGHTH EDITION

ᛒᛒ

Martha Kolln
The Pennsylvania State University

Robert Funk
Eastern Illinois University

Longman

New York San Francisco Boston
London Toronto Sydney Tokyo Singapore Madrid
Mexico City Munich Paris Cape Town Hong Kong Montreal

3 4 5 6 7 8 9 10—BRR—11 10 09

ISBN 10: 0-205-62688-2
ISBN 13: 0-205-62688-5

Longman
is an imprint of

www.pearsonhighered.com

Contents

Preface xi

Chapter 1
Grammar, Usage, and Language Change 1

GRAMMATICALITY 1
Exercise 1.1 Determining Grammatical Structure 2

VARIETIES OF ENGLISH 3
Exercise 1.2 Identifying Lexical Differences 3

REGIONALISMS 5
Exercise 1.3 Recognizing Regional Dialects 5

LANGUAGE CHANGE 7
Exercise 1.4 Examining Changes in English 7

Exercise 1.5 Investigating Changes in Words 9

Chapter 2
An Introduction to Words and Phrases 11

WORD CLASSES 11
Exercise 2.1 Identifying Form-Class Words 13

THE NOUN PHRASE 15
Exercise 2.2 Identifying Noun Phrases 17

THE PREPOSITIONAL PHRASE 19
Exercise 2.3 Identifying Prepositional Phrases 21

Exercise 2.4 Composing with Words and Phrases 23

Chapter 3
Sentence Patterns and Types 25

SLOT BOUNDARIES AND SENTENCE PATTERNS 25
Exercise 3.1 Identifying and Diagramming the Sentence Patterns 27

LINKING VERBS 29

    Exercise 3.2 Identifying Linking Verbs and Other Patterns 30

    Exercise 3.3 Identifying More Sentence Patterns 31

PHRASAL VERBS 33

    Exercise 3.4 Identifying and Diagramming Phrasal Verbs 34

TYPES OF SENTENCES 35

    Exercise 3.5 Identifying Sentences Types and Purposes 35

    Test Exercise 3.6 Identifying Slot Boundaries and Sentence

      Patterns 37

Chapter 4
Understanding Verbs 39

THE VERB-EXPANSION RULE 39

    Exercise 4.1 Identifying Verb Strings 41

    Exercise 4.2 Practicing with Verbs 43

REGULAR AND IRREGULAR VERBS 45

    Exercise 4.3 Choosing the Appropriate Past Tense 46

TROUBLESOME VERBS: *Lie/Lay, Rise/Raise, Sit/Set* 47

    Exercise 4.4 Using the Standard Verb Form 48

    Test Exercise 4.5 Identifying Sentence Patterns and Verb Components 49

Chapter 5
Changing Sentence Focus 51

THE PASSIVE VOICE 51

    Exercise 5.1 Transforming Active Sentences to Passive 53

CHANGING PASSIVE TO ACTIVE 55

    Exercise 5.2 Changing Passive Sentences to Active 57

    Exercise 5.3 Changing the Voice of Sentences 59

THE *THERE* TRANSFORMATION 61
>   Exercise 5.4 Exploring the Use of the *There* Transformation 62

CLEFT SENTENCES 63
>   Exercise 5.5 Using Cleft Sentences 63

>   Test Exercise 5.6 Identifying Shifts in Focus 65

Chapter 6
Modifiers of the Verb: Adverbials 67

>   Exercise 6.1 Recognizing Adverbials 68

>   Exercise 6.2 Identifying and Diagramming Adverbials 71

>   Exercise 6.3 Combining Sentences with Adverbial Clauses 73

>   Exercise 6.4 Prepositional and Infinitive Phrases 75

>   Exercise 6.5 Composing with Adverbials 77

>   Test Exercise 6.6 Identifying Form and Function 79

Chapter 7
Modifiers of the Noun: Adjectivals 81

THE DETERMINER 81
>   Exercise 7.1 Identifying Determiners and Noun Phrases 82

THE PREPOSITIONAL PHRASE 83
>   Exercise 7.2 Identifying and Diagramming Prepositional Phrases 84

THE ADJECTIVAL CLAUSE 85

PUNCTUATING ADJECTIVAL CLAUSES 86
>   Exercise 7.3 Identifying and Punctuating Adjectival Clauses 87

THE PARTICIPIAL PHRASE 89
>   Exercise 7.4 Practicing with Participles 90

>   Exercise 7.5 Identifying and Diagramming Postnoun Modifiers 93

>   Exercise 7.6 Revising Adjectival Clauses 95

DANGLING MODIFIERS 97

    Exercise 7.7 Revising Dangling Modifers 97

MODIFIER PLACEMENT 99

    Exercise 7.8 Revising Misplaced Modifers 99

    Test Exercise 7.9 Form and Function 101

Chapter 8
The Noun Phrase Slots: Nominals 103

    Exercise 8.1 Composing and Using Noun Phrases 103

APPOSITIVES 105

    Exercise 8.2 Using Appositives 105

FORMS OF NOMINALS 107
NOMINAL VERB PHRASES 107

    Exercise 8.3 Understanding Nominal Verb Phrases 109

    Exercise 8.4 Understanding *To*-Phrases 111

NOMINAL CLAUSES 113

    Exercise 8.5 Identifying and Diagramming Nominal Clauses 114

EMBEDDING 117

    Exercise 8.6 Identifying Embedded Nominals 117

    Exercise 8.7 Identifying Dependent Clauses 119

    Exercise 8.8 Nominals and Sentence Patterns 121

    Exercise 8.9 Identifying Nominal Form and Function 123

    Test Exercise 8.10 Identifying Form and Function 125

Chapter 9
Sentence Modifiers 127

    Exercise 9.1 Punctuating Sentence Modifiers 128

    Exercise 9.2 Using Subordinate Clauses 129

ELLIPTICAL CLAUSES 131

    Exercise 9.3 Recognizing and Revising Elliptical Clauses 131

    Exercise 9.4 Adding Absolute Phrases 133

    Test Exercise 9.5 Identifying Form and Function 135

Chapter 10
Coordination 137

    Exercise 10.1 Adding Coordinate Elements 137

PARALLEL STRUCTURE 139

    Exercise 10.2 Identifying Correlatives 140

    Exercise 10.3 Revising for Parallel Structure 141

    Exercise 10.4 Using Conjunctive Adverbs 143

PUNCTUATION OF COORDINATE ELEMENTS 145

    Exercise 10.5 Punctuating Coordinate Structures 146

Chapter 11
Words and Word Classes 147

INFLECTION AND DERIVATION 147

    Exercise 11.1 Derivational Suffixes 148

    Exercise 11.2 Using Bases and Affixes 149

    Exercise 11.3 Form Classes and Inflectional Endings 151

HOMONYMS 153

    Exercise 11.4 Homonymic Suffixes 153

HOMOPHONES 155

    Exercise 11.5 Choosing the Right Homophone 155

HETERONYMS 157

    Exercise 11.6 Identifying Heteronyms 157

STRUCTURE-CLASS WORDS 159

    Exercise 11.7 Identifying Structure-Class Words 159

Exercise 11.8 Recognizing Word Classifications 161

PRONOUNS 163

Exercise 11.9 Using Clear Pronouns 163

Test Exercise 11.10 Identifying Word Classes 165

Chapter 12
Purposeful Punctuation 167

Exercise 12.1 Making Connections and Marking Boundaries 168

Exercise 12.2 Signaling Levels of Importance and Adding Emphasis 169

Exercise 12.3 Punctuating Sentences 171

Answers to the Exercises 173

Preface

This new edition of *Exercises for Understanding English Grammar* follows the goals and design of the previous editions: to provide additional practice and supplemental instruction for users of *Understanding English Grammar*. The exercises in this book will enable students to reinforce their grasp of basic concepts, to extend and explore their understanding, and to apply their knowledge to their writing.

Designed to accompany *Understanding English Grammar*, 8th Edition, this edition of *Exercises* follows the organization of that text. Some of the exercises replicate the format of those in the main text, but many take a different approach, challenging students to demonstrate their grammatical competence by combining, composing, and revising sentences. Although most of the chapters review key points and provide additional examples, students are expected to learn grammatical principles by studying the parent text itself. References to the sentence patterns and sentence slots, for example, depend upon the information in Chapter 3 of *Understanding English Grammar*.

This new edition has been thoroughly revised. Most of the exercises have been extensively rewritten and updated; several have been redesigned. New review materials and exercises have been added to reflect the revised content of the parent text: discussions and exercises on varieties of English and regional dialects (in Chapter 1); a composing exercise involving words and phrases (Chapter 2); and a review of sentence types and purposes (Chapter 3). In addition, there are explanations and exercises about irregular verbs and frequently misused verbs (Chapter 4); an innovative activity on the use of "existential *there*" (Chapter 5); fresh and entertaining items about dangling and misplaced modifiers (Chapter 7); a discussion and exercise on embedded nominals (Chapter 8); further material on correlative conjunctions (Chapter 10); new exercises on homophones and word classifications (Chapter 11); more sentences and passages for applying the rules of punctuation (Chapter 12).

We have retained the self-instructional feature of *Exercises for Understanding English Grammar* by including the answers to the the odd-numbered items for the exercises. We do not supply answers for the composing and sentence-combining exercises, but we do offer suggested responses for exercises that involve revising faulty sentences. Chapters 4 through 9 and 11 also have summary "test" exercises at the end, for which no answers are included. Answers that are not given here can be found in the accompanying Answer Key.

We think that *Exercises for Understanding English Grammar* will provide valuable support for you and your students. We are grateful for the helpful comments of Rebecca Argall, University of Memphis; Rosemary Buck, Eastern Illinois University; Dennis Burges, Longwood University; John Hagge, Iowa State University; Leon Heaton, University of Memphis; Duangrudi Suksang, Eastern Illinois University; and Beth Rapp Young, University of Central Florida at Orlando. We welcome further criticisms and suggestions for making this book even more useful to you.

Martha Kolln and Robert

Chapter 1

Grammar, Usage, and Language Change

As the Introduction to Part I of *Understanding English Grammar* points out, you are already an expert in using your native language. You have the competence both to create and to understand sentences that you have never heard or read. If you have reached this point on the page and understood what you have read, you "know" English grammar.

The five exercises in this first chapter are designed to help you explore your innate understanding of grammar: to recognize some basic principles of sentence structure, to examine some variations of English, and to look at the way that the language changes.

GRAMMATICALITY

Your knowledge of grammar is something you developed with little conscious effort as a child. You learned how to put words together in the right order, and you acquired the ability to recognize when a string of words is not grammatical. For example, read the following sentences and rate them according to their acceptability:

1. Old this wooden shack is over falling almost.

2. This wooden old shack is falling almost over.

3. This old wooden shack is almost falling over.

Chances are you have rated them, in order of acceptability, 3, 2, and 1. If you examine why you accepted the third and rejected the first, you will discover some rules that are part of your language competence—rules about word order and movability.

Exercise 1.1
Determining Grammatical Structure

A sentence is grammatical if it conforms to the way native speakers structure their language. A sentence may not always follow the usages prescribed for **standard English**, but it is still considered grammatical by the speakers who regularly use it.

Directions: Identify the following sentences as grammatical or ungrammatical. For the sentences you think are ungrammatical, rearrange the words to make them grammatical (use only the words given). It might be possible to make more than one grammatical arrangement.

1. Pizza for dinner we're having.

   _____

2. He gave a call his friend best.

   _____

3. Who are you looking for?

   _____

4. Ring bells loudly the.

   _____

5. Ran out soccer players eleven onto the field.

   _____

6. I don't trust nobody.

   _____

7. Tiny your kittens three are very.

   _____

8. Ontogeny recapitulates phylogeny.

   _____

VARIETIES OF ENGLISH

English is the majority first language in twenty-three countries; it is the official language or the joint official language in almost fifty countries. The number of first-language speakers of English worldwide has been estimated at well over 300 million, more than 220 million of them living in the United States. As a result of this geographical spread, English has undergone numerous changes in various parts of the world. There are clear distinctions among British English, American English, Canadian English, Australian English, and so on. These varities of English retain enough structural similiarity not to be considered separate languages, but they can differ greatly in pronunciation and vocabulary.

Exercise 1.2
Identifying Lexical Differences

Directions: Following is a list of words from British or Canadian English that are not used in American English or that have a very different meaning from the way the words are used in the United States. Find a word from American English that means the same thing as each word in the list. Try making a guess first; then use a dictionary and look for the definitions labeled "chiefly British" or something similar.

1. lorry   American English:

2. solicitor (legal)   American English:

3. chemist   American English:

4. football   American English:

5. torch   American English:

6. bonnet (a car part)   American English:

7. crisps   American English:

8. serviette   American English:

9. riding   American English:

10. plimsolls   American English:

11. queue   American English:

12. lift   American English:

13. chesterfield   American English:

14. spanner   American English:

15. biscuit   American English:

REGIONALISMS

Each of the many national varieties of English can be further subdivided into regional dialects. Despite the mobility of people in the United States and the influence of national advertising and media broadcasts, regional differences in American English persist. Speakers in the southern part of the country speak differently from speakers in the Rocky Mountain states—or in New England or the Midwest. Dialectical distinctions occur within these regions as well. Everyone speaks a dialect, although we tend to think that it's other people who "talk different." Move to another part of the country, or state, and you will discover that *you* are the one with the dialect.

Exercise 1.3
Recognizing Regional Dialects

A. *Directions:* For each of the following, give the term you are most likely to use or would expect to hear in your home region.

1. Where do you get water from?   a. tap, b. faucet, c. spigot

2. What do you call a carbonated soft drink?   a. soda, b. soda pop, c. pop, d. soft drink, e. sodie

3. What do you fry eggs in?   a. fry pan, b. skillet, c. frying pan

4. What might you eat for breakfast?   a. hotcakes, b. flapjackets, c. pancakes

5. What do you carry water in?   a. bucket, b. pail

6. What do you call a sandwich made on a long roll and containing a variety of meats and cheeses?   a. hoagie, b. submarine, c. grinder, d. hero, e. poor boy

7. What do you call the evening meal?   a. supper, b. dinner

8. What do you call a limited-access, high-speed road without traffic lights or crossroads? a. freeway, b. expressway, c. interstate, d. turnpike, e. parkway

9. What term do you use for unauthorized absence from school?   a. play hooky, b. bag school, c. skip school, d. ditch school

10. What do you call the container for carrying groceries from the store? a. bag, b. sack, c. tote, d. poke

B. *Directions:* In each of the following, identify the expressions you use or are most likely to hear in your home region.

1. the floor needs swept; the floor needs to be swept; the floor needs sweeping

2. we stood in line; we stood on line

3. quarter to six; quarter till six; quarter of six; quarter before six

4. sick to your stomach; sick at your stomach

5. she isn't at home; she isn't home; she isn't to home

6. he's waiting for you; he's waiting on you

7. they hadn't ought to do that; they oughn't to do that; they shouldn't do that

8. she graduated high school; she graduated from high school

Compare your answers with those of your classmates. Do the differences surprise you, or were you already aware of them? Have you heard other members of your family or community use any of these terms or expressions? How old are they? Where do they live?

LANGUAGE CHANGE

For the most part, language changes because society changes. And while such change is inevitable, it is rarely predictable. Although some people see it as a sign of deterioration or decay, language change occurs so infrequently and so slowly that it seldom causes problems in communication or precision. Most change affects the lexicon (vocabulary) of a language: New words are added and others change meaning or acquire additional meanings. Changes in sentence structure are less frequent and take much longer to develop.

Exercise 1.4
Examining Changes in English

Directions: Translate these passages from Shakespeare's *Julius Caesar* and *Hamlet* into modern English and explain the grammatical changes you found it necessary to make.

1. Looks it not like the king?

2. Wherefore rejoice? What conquests brings he home?

3. To thine own self be true. . .Thou canst not then be false to any man.

4. This was the most unkindest cut of all.

5. Think not, thou noble Roman. / That ever Brutus will go bound to Rome.

6. But whilt thou hear me how I did proceed?

7. What dost thou with thy best apparel on?

Exercise 1.5

Investigating Changes in Words

Directions: The meanings of words change, and the meaning a word once had may have little or no bearing on its meaning today. For example, the word *nice* used to mean "ignorant" or "foolish," but now it means "generally pleasing" or "carefully discerning." Check out the origins and history of the following terms in the *Oxford English Dictionary* or another book of word origins. What did the word used to mean? How has that meaning changed?

1. sail [*verb*]

2. holiday

3. starve

4. meat

5. angel

6. vulgar

7. hussy

8. bonfire

9. stupid

10. minister

11. alibi

12. decimate

Chapter 2

An Introduction to Words and Phrases

Grammar is the study of how sentences are put together. The exercises in this chapter will give you practice in identifying and understanding the basic components of sentences—words and phrases. This practice will also lay the groundwork for the study of sentence patterns and sentence types in the chapters that follow.

WORD CLASSES

Sentences are, of course, made up of words. Traditional grammarians classified these words into eight categories, called *the parts of speech,* in order to make their description of English conform to the word categories of Latin grammar. More recently, however, linguists have looked closely at English and now classify words according to their form and their function in the sentence.

The four major classes of words in English are the *form-class words:* nouns, verbs, adjectives, and adverbs. These words provide the primary content in a sentence. Learning to identify form-class words will help you to understand how sentences are put together.

The key feature of form-class words is that they change form. They have endings (or spelling changes) that make specific grammatical distinctions.

Nouns

- have singular and plural forms: dog/dogs; woman/women.

- change form to show possession: the *dog's* owner; *women's* rights.

- are marked or signaled by articles (*a, an, the*) or other determiners: *a* dog, *that* woman, *my* pet, *some* people.

Verbs

- have present-tense and past-tense forms: bark/barked; buy/bought.

- have an -*s* form and an -*ing* form: barks/barking; buys/buying.

Adjectives

- have comparative and superlative forms: happy/happier/happiest; expensive/more expensive/most expensive.

- can be qualified by words like *very* and *too:* very happy, too expensive.

Adverbs

- have comparative and superlative forms: soon/sooner/soonest; carefully/more carefully/most carefully.

- can be qualified by words like *very* and *too:* very carefully, too soon.

- are often formed by adding *-ly* to adjectives: expensive → expensively; happy → happily.

We can distinguish adjectives from adverbs in three ways:

1. Most adjectives fit into both blanks of this "adjective test frame":

   The _____ NOUN is very _____.

   The *happy* wanderer is very *happy.*

   The *expensive* necklace is very *expensive.*

2. Adverbs are often movable:

   The dogs barked *frequently.*

   The dogs *frequently* barked.

   Frequently the dogs barked.

3. Adverbs can usually be identified by the information they provide: They tell *when, where, why, how,* and *how often.*

Exercise 2.1

Identifying Form-Class Words

A. ***Directions:*** Identify the form class of the underlined words in the following sentences as noun, verb, adjective, or adverb. Indicate the characteristics of form that you used to make your identification.

Example:

A ten-ton elephant <u>weighs</u> less than a <u>whale</u>.

weighs: verb—present tense, -s form; other forms would be weighed, weighing

whale: noun—marked by *a*; plural form would be whales

1. The sperm whale <u>stays</u> underwater for thirty minutes at a <u>time</u>.

2. Most whales <u>come</u> to the <u>surface</u> more <u>often</u>.

3. The <u>waters</u> of the Antarctic Ocean provide an <u>abundant</u> supply of plankton for these giant <u>creatures</u>.

4. A <u>small</u> <u>blue</u> whale <u>eats</u> as many as twenty-four seals every day.

5. These <u>huge</u> mammals <u>sometimes</u> leap from the water just for fun.

6. Their tails <u>align</u> <u>horizontally</u> with their <u>bodies</u>.

B. *Directions:* Underline all the nouns, verbs, adjectives, and adverbs in the following sentences. Identify the class of each by writing one of these labels below the word: N, V, adj, or adv.

1. The new contestant appeared nervous.

2. The famous host played shamelessly to the audience.

3. Many members of the crowd dutifully applauded his inane remarks.

4. The director often interrupts the program with insincere encouragement.

5. The astute critics panned the show mercilessly.

THE NOUN PHRASE

The most common word group in the sentence, one that fills many roles in the sentence patterns, is the **noun phrase** (NP), consisting of a noun **headword** together with its modifiers. As you may remember, the word *noun* is from the Latin word for "name"—and that's how nouns are traditionally defined: as the name of a person, place, thing, concept, event, and the like. But an even better way to recognize and understand nouns is to call on your language competence, to apply in a conscious way what you know intuitively about nouns. For example, one feature common to most nouns when we put them in sentences is the **determiner** that signals them:

a pizza

the game on Saturday

every class

those students standing on the corner

several friends from my hometown

four members of our speech team

Tom's friend

that problem

The articles *a* and *the*, demonstrative pronouns like *that* and *those*, possessive pronouns and possessive names like *my* and *our* and *Tom's*, indefinite pronouns like *several* and *every*, and numbers like *four*—all of these are determiners that signal the beginning of a noun phrase. Sometimes other words intervene between the determiner and the headword noun:

several old friends from my hometown

the soccer game on Saturday

a delicious pizza

that recurring problem

In each case, however, you can identify the headword of the noun phrase by asking *what?*

several what? (*friends*)

the what? (*game*)

a what? (*pizza*)

that what? (*problem*)

When you become conscious of determiners, you'll begin to recognize how helpful they can be in discovering the opening of noun phrases.

We should note that there are several kinds of nouns that are not signaled by determiners. For example, proper nouns—the names of particular people, events, places, and the like (*Aunt Bess, President Lincoln, Mt. Rainier, Oklahoma, Main Street, Thanksgiving*)—rarely have determiners; abstract nouns (*happiness, justice*), mass, or noncountable, nouns (*homework, water*), and plural countable nouns (*people, children*) may also appear without them.

Another helpful way to recognize nouns—for example, to distinguish nouns from other word categories—is to recognize the various forms they have. Most nouns have both plural and possessive forms: *book, book's, books, books'; teacher, teacher's, teachers, teachers'; class, class's, classes, classes'*. If you can make a word plural, it's a noun: *two books, three classes, four teachers*. But even those that don't have a plural form, such as proper and abstract and mass nouns, generally do have a possessive form: *Joe's* book, the *water's* strange taste

Exercise 2.2

Identifying Noun Phrases

A. *Directions:* Identify each noun phrase in the following sentences by circling the determiner and underlining the headword.

Example:

The bookstore will hold its annual textbook sale soon.

1. My relatives have many odd habits.

2. Aunt Flo has an extensive collection of old umbrellas.

3. Aunt Flo's umbrella collection decorates her front porch.

4. Her oldest son keeps a pet mongoose in the garage.

5. My older brother built a geodesic dome for his second wife.

6. Our cousins from Atlanta make an annual pilgrimage to the Mojave Desert.

7. Their maternal grandmother dresses her three small dogs in colorful sweaters.

8. Uncle Silas's son plays the kazoo in a marching band.

9. This eccentric behavior rarely causes problems with the neighbors.

10. Some members of the family never attend the annual family reunion.

B. *Directions:* The opening noun phrase in each of the ten sentences of Exercise 2.2A functions as the subject. When you substitute a personal pronoun for that noun phrase (*I, you, he, she, it, we, they*), you can easily identify the line between the subject and predicate. The pronoun stands in for the entire noun phrase, not just the headword.

Underline the subject noun phrase. In the space provided, identify the pronoun that could replace it.

Example:

   It   The bookstore will hold its annual textbook sale soon.

_____ 1. My relatives have many odd habits.

_____ 2. Aunt Flo has an extensive collection of old umbrellas.

_____ 3. Aunt Flo's umbrella collection decorates her front porch.

_____ 4. Her oldest son keeps a pet mongoose in the garage.

_____ 5. My older brother built a geodesic dome for his second wife.

_____ 6. Our cousins from Atlanta make an annual pilgrimage to the Mojave Desert.

_____ 7. Their maternal grandmother dresses her three small dogs in colorful sweaters.

_____ 8. Uncle Silas's son plays the kazoo in a marching band.

_____ 9. This eccentric behavior rarely causes problems with the neighbors.

_____ 10. Some members of the family never attend the annual family reunion.

THE PREPOSITIONAL PHRASE

The second kind of phrase we will examine is the prepositional phrase, a word group that shows up throughout the sentence, sometimes as a part of a noun phrase and sometimes as a modifier of the verb. The prepositional phrase consists of a **preposition** and its **object**, which is usually a noun phrase.

In the following three noun phrases, which you saw in Exercise 2.2, the noun headword is shown in bold; the underlined word group that follows the headword in each case is a **prepositional phrase**:

an extensive **collection** of old umbrellas

our **cousins** from Atlanta

an annual **pilgrimage** to the Mojave Desert

The prepositional phrase is one of our most common ways of modifying a noun, in order to add details or to make clear the identity of the noun:

that **house** near the corner

their **reports** about the Civil War

the **man** with the camera

a **ticket** for the concert

You'll note that in each of these examples, there's a noun phrase embedded as a modifier in another phrase.

In the foregoing prepositional phrases, we have seen the following **prepositions**: *of, from, to, near, about, with,* and *for.* In Chapter 13 of *Understanding English Grammar,* there is a list of about fifty more, all of which are among the most common words in the English language—words we use automatically every day. Some prepositions consist of more than one word. Among them are *according to, because of, except for, instead of, on account of,* and *in spite of.* It would be a good idea at this point to become familiar with all the possibilities.

When prepositional phrases modify nouns, they are functioning the way that adjectives do, so we call them **adjectivals.** When they modify verbs, they are functioning as adverbs do, so we call them **adverbials.** Like adverbs, they tell *when, where, how, why,* and *how often:*

My sister has developed some strange allergies in recent years.

In the fall my brother usually gets hay fever.

As you see, these adverbials are identical in form to the adjectival prepositional phrases: a preposition followed by a noun phrase. But the adverbial ones can be moved around in their sentences:

In recent years my sister has developed some strange allergies.

My brother usually gets hay fever in the fall.

This movability is an important difference between the two functions: The adjectival prepositional phrase cannot be moved from its position following the noun it modifies. Not every adverbial is movable either, but if a prepositional phrase can be moved, it is clearly adverbial.

Sometimes we use an adjectival prepositional phrase to identify or describe the object of another preposition:

Our excursion took us into the backwoods of West Virginia.

adj

adv

The postmark on this letter from my niece says Bonn, Germany.

adj

adj

Exercise 2.3
Identifying Prepositional Phrases

Directions: Underline the prepositional phrases in the following sentences and identify them as adjectival (adj) or adverbial (adv). (Note: Remember to call on your knowledge of pronouns in deciding if a prepositional phrase is part of a noun phrase. In the example, we could substitute *they* for the subject because it would replace "Many industries from the United States." When a prepositional phrase is part of a noun phrase, it is, by definition, adjectival.)

Example:

Many industries <u>from the United States</u> have built manufacturing
adj

plants <u>in Mexico</u> <u>in recent years</u>.
adv   adv

1. Many paths lead to the top of the mountain.

2. Leonard Bernstein became the assistant conductor of the New York Philharmonic Orchestra in 1943.

3. On a cold November afternoon, the Prince of Patagonia met me at his public relations firm.

4. According to Mark Twain life on a riverboat was an opportunity for adventure.

5. The students from my study group take long walks around the campus on sunny days.

6. In spite of my allergy to dairy products, I still eat yogurt on a daily basis.

7. The student assistant in our botany class made a presentation about wild turkeys.

8. During the night our dog cornered a skunk behind the garage.

9. Talent contests with elimination rounds are the most popular shows on television.

10. Because of my poor attendance record, the new provost invited me to her office for a chat.

Exercise 2.4

Composing with Words and Phrases

Directions: Expand these core sentences by adding adjectives, adverbs, and prepositional phrases, both adjectival and adverbial. Underline your additions and label them **adj** (for adjective/adjectival) and **adv** (for adverb/adverbial).

    Example: The hound growls

The <u>mangy</u> <u>old</u> hound <u>on our front porch</u> growls <u>feebly</u> <u>at every passing stranger.</u>
     adj   adj   adj   adv   adv

1. The party was a flop.

2. The batter struck out.

3. The president makes decisions.

4. The children danced.

5. A creature emerged.

6. I washed three sweaters.

Chapter 3

Sentence Patterns and Types

The exercises in this chapter provide practice in recognizing and analyzing the basic **sentence patterns** and their parts—the focus of Chapter 3 in *Understanding English Grammar.*

SLOT BOUNDARIES AND SENTENCE PATTERNS

In the followwing exercises you will be identifying slot boundaries and sentence patterns. Following are detailed steps that will lead you to the answers. Here's an example:

My roommates made a delicious meatloaf on Tuesday.

Step 1: Separate the subject and the predicate. The subject is the *who* or *what* that the sentence is about. In this example, it's *My roommates.* You can figure out that the subject noun phrase encompasses just those two words by substituting a pronoun:

<u>They</u> made a delicious meatloaf on Tuesday.

Don't forget, however, that sometimes an adverbial occupies the opening slot. You can identify adverbials by their movability. But in figuring out the sentence pattern, you should ignore them—they're optional.

Step 2: You'll recall that it's the predicate that determines the sentence pattern. First, of course, you must identify *made* as the predicating verb. One way to do that is to recognize *made* as an action—but that doesn't always work: Verbs are not always actions, and action words are not always verbs. In your study of verbs in Chapter 4 of *Understanding English Grammar* you'll discover that the predicating verb is the sentence slot that can have auxiliaries of various kinds. You can use that understanding to figure out that *made* is a verb by asking yourself, "Could I also say *has made* or *is making* or *might make*? " If the answer is *yes,* then you know that *made* is the predicating verb.

Step 3: How many slots follow the predicating verb? And what is the form of the word or word group that fills each slot? The word group following the verb *made* is a noun phrase, *a delicious meatloaf.* Here the opening article, *a,* is the clue: Words like *a* and *the* and *my,* the determiners, are noun signalers. When you see a determiner, you're at the beginning of a noun phrase (NP). And where does the NP end? You can prove that *on Tuesday* has its own slot by testing the boundaries of the meatloaf phrase: Substitute a pronoun:

My roommates made <u>it</u> on Tuesday.

Clearly, *on Tuesday* has its own slot: It's an adverbial telling *when*. (It's not an "on Tuesday meat-loaf"!) You could also give it the movability test: It could just as easily—and grammatically—open the sentence.

On Tuesday my roommates made a delicious meatloaf.

Step 4. What is the sentence pattern? Because *a delicious meatloaf* and *my roommates* have different referents, the NPs in the formula have different numbers:

NP_1 Verb NP_2 (Adverbial)

And because *on Tuesday* is optional (the sentence is grammatical without it), you'll discover that the sentence pattern is VII.

Remember that the sentence patterns are differentiated by their verbs: *be*, linking, intransitive, and transitive. The four transitive patterns (VII to X) are subdivided on the basis of their verbs too. A verb with a meaning like "give" will have an indirect object as well as a direct object; and those two objects, you'll recall, have different referents:

Pattern VIII

The teacher gave <u>the students</u> <u>an assignment</u>.
               ind obj   dir obj

Some verbs will take both a direct object and an object complement—either an adjective (Pattern IX) or a noun phrase (Pattern X). In the case of Pattern X, the two NPs in the predicate have the same referent:

Pattern IX

The students consider <u>their teacher</u> <u>fair</u>.
                      dir obj   obj comp

Pattern X

The students consider <u>their teacher</u> <u>a fair person</u>.
                      dir obj   obj comp

(Reminder: A chart of the ten sentence patterns is displayed on the endpapers inside the book's cover.)

Exercise 3.1

Identifying and Diagramming the Sentence Patterns

Directions: Draw vertical lines to identify the slot boundaries in the following sentences; label each slot according to its form and function. In the parentheses following the sentence, identify its sentence pattern:

Example:

My roommates | made | a delicious meatloaf | on Tuesday. __(VII)__

Form:	NP	V	NP	prep phr
Function:	subj	pred vb	dir obj	adv

Then, on separate paper, diagram the sentences. When you identify the sentence pattern, you establish the shape of the diagram. The main line of the diagram will look like the skeletal model for that pattern shown in Chapter 3 of *Understanding English Grammar.*

1. Tryouts for the spring musical begin in a few days. (_____)

2. The director posted the casting call yesterday. (_____)

3. My girlfriend is extremely nervous about her audition. (_____)

4. She once played the part of Maria in *West Side Story.* (_____)

5. Her parents consider that performance a great theatrical triumph. (_____)

6. A freshman from Chicago is everybody's pick for the male lead. (_____)

7. My roommate remains confident of his chances. (_____)

8. The other competitors are usually in the audience. (_____)

9. They graciously give their fellow actors a hearty round of applause. (_____)

10. The unsuccessful aspirants often become members of the technical crew. (_____)

LINKING VERBS

Patterns IV and V contain linking verbs other than *be*. *Be* is the most frequently used linking verb in English; it also has more forms and variations than other verbs. For these reasons, we have separated it from the other linking verbs to emphasize its special qualities.

Linking verbs connect the *subject* with a *subject complement*, a word or phrase that follows the verb and completes the meaning of the sentence. In Pattern IV, the subject complement is an adjective that describes or names an attribute of the subject. In Pattern V, the subject complement is a noun phrase that renames or identifies the subject—the NPs have the same referent.

A small number of verbs fit into these linking patterns. The common ones can be roughly divided into three categories:

- Verbs that express a change in state: *become, get, grow, turn,* etc.

- Verbs that express existence or appearance: *appear, seem, remain, stay*

- Verbs of perception: *look, feel, taste, smell, sound*

In addition to the limited number of common linking verbs, others not usually thought of as linking can, on occasion, be followed by an adjective and therefore fit into Pattern IV:

The screw *worked* loose.

The witness *stood* firm.

The well *ran* dry.

Very few verbs fit in Pattern V. The most common are *become* and *remain*; sometimes *seem, make, continue,* and *stay* will also take noun phrases as subject complements.

Most of the linking verbs listed here can also occur in other sentence patterns. You can often test for a linking verb by substituting a form of *be, seem,* or *become* in the sentence:

The screw *worked* loose = The screw *became* loose.

My uncle *remained* a bachelor = My uncle *was* a bachelor.

The meaning may change a little, but if the substitution produces a grammatical sentence, then you know you have a linking verb. Of course, the easiest way to recognize linking verbs is to identify the subject complement and understand its relationship to the subject.

Exercise 3.2

Identifying Linking Verbs and Other Patterns

Directions: Decide if the verbs in the following sentences are linking, intransitive, or transitive. Then write the sentence pattern number in the parentheses after each sentence.

1. The weather turned cool over the weekend. (_____)

2. The committee members turned their attention to the next item on the agenda. (____).

3. The Schillers remained our neighbors for many years. (_____)

4. The class grew impatient with the teacher's rambling explanation. (_____)

5. My nephew grew a goatee in two months.

6. The audience stayed awake through the whole speech. (_____)

7. A panel of judges stayed the execution. (_____)

8. The children stayed in their room.

9. Bill's younger sister makes delicious lasagna. (_____)

10. She will make a great chef someday. (_____)

11. This juice tastes bitter. (_____)

12. The detective tasted traces of cyanide in the juice. (____)

13. During last night's thunderstorm we went to the basement. (_____)

14. The company went bankrupt last year. (_____)

15. The child fell ill during the night. (_____)

16. No snowflake falls in the wrong place. [Zen saying] (_____)

17. Men have become the tools of their tools. [Henry David Thoreau] (_____)

Exercise 3.3
Identifying More Sentence Patterns

Directions: Draw vertical lines to identify the slot boundaries in the following sentences; label each slot according to its form and function. In the parentheses following the sentence, identify its sentence pattern. Your instructor may want you to diagram these sentences on separate paper.

Example:

On its driest day, | the Susquehanna River | provides |
prep phr   NP   V
adv   subj   pred vb

one billion gallons of fresh water | to the Chesapeake Bay. (VII)
NP   prep phr
dir obj   adv

1. You nearly sideswiped that squad car across the street. (_____)

2. The police are at the door. (_____)

3. The air always seems fresh and clean after a spring rain. (_____)

4. In the first few decades of the twentieth century, Sears sold houses through its catalogue. (____)

5. Thousands of families in the Midwest still live in Sears houses. (_____)

6. The barista at the new Starbucks in town was once a contestant on *Deal or No Deal.*
   (_____)

7. During rush hour my new car sputtered and stalled in the middle of a busy intersection. (_____)

8. With further practice, Jeanne will become an extraordinary gymnast. (_____)

9. The exchange student from Naples fixed our soccer team a traditional Sicilian meal.
   (_____)

10. Monica's friends consider her new boyfriend a big improvement over the last one.
    (_____)

11. The candidate made her position on healthcare very clear. (_____)

12. Her ambitious plan includes universal coverage and a hefty tax hike. (_____)

PHRASAL VERBS

In your study of the sentence patterns you learned about the **particle**, a word that combines with a verb to form a **phrasal verb**. In the following example, *up* is a particle:

Pat looked up the word.

The phrasal verb *look up* has a distinctive meaning, one that is different from the combined meanings of *look* and *up*. In contrast, *up* is a preposition in this sentence:

Pat looked up the hall.

Here's a slot analysis of the two:

Pat | looked up | the word. (Pattern VII)
Form: N   vb   NP
Function: subj   pred vb   dir obj

Pat | looked | up the hall. (Pattern VI)
Form: N   vb   prep phr
Function: subj   pred vb   adv

And here is what they look like when diagrammed:

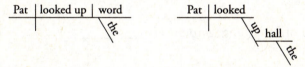

We could also say "Pat looked up," where *up* is an adverb:

Exercise 3.4

Identifying and Diagramming Phrasal Verbs

Directions: Draw vertical lines to show the slot boundaries in the following sentences, paying particular attention to the verbs. In the parentheses following the sentence, identify the number of the sentence pattern.

Example:

The police | are looking into | the suspect's activities. _(VII)_

(Helpful hint: One way to test a phrasal verb is to substitute a single word that means the same thing. Often you can find a synonym. In the previous example, we could substitute *investigating* for *looking into*.)

1.   The ski lift shut down for the summer. (_____)

2.   The job candidate turned down the offer. (_____)

3.   The fugitive fled down the alley. (_____)

4.   The couple called off their engagement. (_____)

5.   The defendant stood by her story. (_____)

6.   The bailiff stood by the door. (_____)

7.   The prosecutor suddenly stood up. (_____)

8.   His mother-in-law looks after the children on weekends. (_____)

9.   I looked for my keys everywhere. (_____)

10.   They put up with the children's rowdy behavior. (_____)

On separate paper diagram the ten sentences you just analyzed. Remember that all the words that make up the verb will be in the verb slot on the main line, as you saw in the diagram of "Pat looked up the word."

TYPES OF SENTENCES

The sentence patterns you've been studying are classified according to what kind of verbs they contain—being, linking, intransitive, transitive. We can also classify sentences according to their purpose or function.

- n **Declarative** sentences make statements and follow a subject-verb-complement pattern: *Nobody saw us. Reynard is the best candidate.* The majority of sentences in English are declarative.

- n **Interrogative** sentences ask questions and usually involve a subject-verb inversion (where the verb or auxiliary verb comes before the subject): *Did anyone see us? Who is your choice for president?*

- n **Imperative** sentences give commands and have no subject (although *you* is implied as the subject): *Look over there. Vote for Reynard for president.*

- n **Exclamatory** sentences express surprise, anger, or excitement. This type of sentence gives special attention to a complement by shifting it to the front of the sentence and introducing it with What or How: *What a lousy candidate he is! How observant you are!*

Exercise 3.5

Identifying Sentence Types and Purposes

A. *Directions:* On the line after each of the following sentences identify its type: declarative, imperative, interrogative, or exclamatory. In the parentheses, write the number of the sentence pattern.

> **Example:**　　I asked you a question. <u>declarative</u>　(VIII)
> 　　　　　　　　Be careful out there. 　<u>imperative</u>　(II)

1. Betty's cats eat potato chips. _____ (　)

2. Pick up those dirty socks. _____ (　)

3. Tell me your name again. _____ (　)

4. What is your name? _____ (　)

5. What a terrific movie that was! _____ (　)

6. Is skydiving safe? _____ (　)

7. The parachute finally opened. _____ (   )

8. How calm you seem. _____ (   )

9. Consider yourself lucky. _____ (   )

10. Have you ever been to Europe? _____ (   )

B. Directions: From each of the following noun-verb pairs, create a statement, a question, and a command.

Example: water, boil
          Statement: Water boils at 212 degrees Fahrenheit.
          Question: Is the water boiling yet?
          Command: Boil some water for our tea.

1. noise, stop

2. email, send

3. computer, use

4. story, tell

Test Exercise 3.6
Identifying Slot Boundaries and Sentence Patterns

Directions: Draw vertical lines to identify the slot boundaries in the following sentences; label each slot according to its form and function. In the parentheses following the sentence, identify its sentence pattern. [Answers are not given.]

Example:

My roommates | fixed | meatloaf and baked potatoes | for dinner | on Tuesday. (VII)
Form: NP   V   compd NP   prep ph   prep ph
Function: subj   pred vb   dir obj   adv   adv

1. After several weeks on the job, Doris and Modelle became best buddies. (_____)

2. The librarian found me a pamphlet and two additional articles. (_____)

3. Eager sunbathers crowded the beaches during the first warm days in May. (_____)

4. Our cat often sits on the widow sill for the whole afternoon. (_____)

5. To the ant, a few drops of rain are a flood. (____)

6. The team leader broke down the major goals into three specific tasks. (____)

7. My great uncle left his wife a sizable fortune. (_____)

8. The new medication left the patient weak and drowsy. (_____)

9. The dean's secretary set up an appointment for me for tomorrow. (_____)

10. My breath smells bad because of the garlic. (_____)

11. The new sales manager is by nature ebullient and friendly. (_____)

12. The pickles are next to the potato salad. (_____)

13. My project director called my last proposal unworkable. (_____)

14. The runner from Morocco tripped and fell at the finish line. (_____)

15. A society of sheep begets a government of wolves. [Bertrand de Jouvenal] (_____)

16. Laughter is the closest thing to the grace of God. [Karl Barth] (_____)

17. The hardness of the butter is proportional to the softness of the bread. (_____)

18. A wide screen makes a bad film worse. [Samuel Goldwyn]. (_____)

19. The FBI looked into the matter. (_____)

20. Too many people make money their primary pursuit. (_____)

Chapter 4

Understanding Verbs

THE VERB-EXPANSION RULE

The formula you studied in Chapter 4 of *Understanding English Grammar*, known as the "verb-expansion rule," represents our system for generating all the possible grammatical verb forms. It explains our system for using auxiliaries:

VP = T (M) (have + -en) (be + -ing) MV

T stands for tense, either present or past. The tense is applied to the first word in the string:

pres + eat = eat(s)

past + eat = ate

present + have + -en + eat = have (has) eaten

past + have + -en + eat = had eaten

M stands for the modal auxiliaries, *can/could, will/would, shall/should, may/might, must, ought to:*

pres + can + eat = can eat

past + can + eat = could eat

pres + may + eat = may eat

past + will + eat = would eat

have + -en: This component of the rule says that when *have* serves as an auxiliary it is followed by the -en form (the past participle) of the main verb (or of the auxiliary *be*):

pres + have + -en + eat = have (has) eaten

past + have + -en + eat = had eaten

pres + have + -en + be + -ing + eat = has (have) been eating

past + have + -en + be + -ing + eat = had been eating

be + -ing: This component of the rule says that when *be* serves as an auxiliary, it is followed by the -ing form of the verb:

pres + be + -ing + eat = is (am, are) eating

past + be + -ing + eat = was (were) eating

past + may + be + -ing + eat = might be eating

MV, the main verb, will always be the last slot in the verb string. Its form will be determined by the auxiliary that precedes it or by **T** if there is no auxiliary:

pres + eat = eats

past + eat = ate

past + be + -ing + eat = was (were) eating

past + shall + eat = should eat

Exercise 4.1

Identifying Verb Strings

Directions: Underline the verb—along with any auxiliaries—in the following sentences. Then show the components of the verb-expansion rule that the verb string contains. Remember that in every case the first component is either present or past tense.

Example:

We <u>have finished</u> our homework.

pres + have + -en + finish _____

(Note that *have + -en* is not shown in parentheses here. The parentheses mean that the auxiliary is optional: We don't have to choose it. Here, however, we are examining what we did choose.)

1. Our team has won its last five games.

   _____

2. Leah is feeling ill today.

   _____

3. My partners and I have been planning our clearance sale.

   _____

4. It could be our biggest event of the year.

   _____

5. We had expected a larger turnout.

   _____

6. We may have been trying too hard.

   _____

7. We now understand the problem.

   _____

8. The boss should give us a day off.

   _____

9. You can be a big help.

   _____

10. The police may have arrested the wrong person.

    _____

Exercise 4.2

Practicing with Verbs

Directions: Turn each of the following strings into a predicating verb; then use it in a sentence with "the students" as the subject.

Example:

pres + will + be + -ing + work

will be working / The students will be working on their projects this weekend. _____

1. past + be + -ing + read

    _____

    _____

2. past + have + -en + take

    _____

    _____

3. past + be + -ing + be

    _____

    _____

4. past + can + have + -en + help

    _____

    _____

5. pres + have + -en + be + -ing + finish

_____

_____

6. past + shall + have + -en + spend

_____

_____

7. past + be + -ing + go

_____

_____

8. pres + will + be + -ing + start

_____

_____

9. past + have + -en + have

_____

_____

10. past + may + have + -en + be + -ing + make

_____

_____

REGULAR AND IRREGULAR VERBS

Most verbs in the English language are **regular**. These verbs consistently add *-d* or *-ed* to the base (sometimes with a spelling change) to get the past tense forms: *type/typed, stop/stopped, try/tried*. The third principal part, the **past participle**, of a regular verb is the same as the past tense.

By contrast, **irregular** verbs do not consistently add *-d* or *-ed* to form the past tense and past participle. They are irregular in a number of ways:

Some change an internal vowel to form the past tense and the past participle: *drink/drank/drunk, sing/sang/sung*.

Others change a vowel for the past tense but add an *-n* ending for the past participle: *see/saw/seen, know/knew/known*.

Some change a vowel for the past tense and use the same form for the past participle: *sit/sat/sat, teach/taught/taught*.

Some others use the base form for all three principal parts: *cut/cut/cut, set/set/set*.

And one verb uses a different word for the past tense: *go/went/gone*.

About two hundred verbs in English are irregular; they are some of the oldest and most commonly used verbs in the language. Since even native speakers are sometimes unsure which form to use with a particular verb, dictionaries and handbooks routinely give the principal parts for irregular verbs.

Some verbs have both a regular and an irregular past or past participle. These two forms are sometimes genuine alternatives: You can use either one without conveying a contrast in meaning or style. But in some cases the forms have separate meanings (people are *hanged*, pictures are *hung*), or one form is more informal (*busted* for *burst*).

Exercise 4.3

Choosing the Appropriate Past Tense

Directions: Look at the underlined verbs in the following pairs of sentences and decide which ones are interchangeable, which ones are used only in a particular context, and which ones are nonstandard. Start by making your own judgments, but then consult a usage dictionary or writer's handbook to check your knowledge and intuition.

1. They <u>pleaded</u> with their daughter to come home again.

   The protestors <u>pled</u> not guilty to the trespassing charges.

2. The sun <u>shone</u> through the kitchen windows.

   On Sundays our father got up early and <u>shined</u> our shoes for us.

3. We <u>sneaked</u> out by the back door.

   We <u>snuck</u> past the desk clerk.

4. The old man carefully <u>wove</u> a complicated gold pattern into the cloth.

   We spotted our friends as they <u>weaved</u> their way through the crowd.

5. For some reason I <u>woke</u> up early.

   The nurse <u>waked</u> him gently.

6. Helicopters <u>flew</u> the accident victims to the hospital.

   The second baseman <u>flied</u> to left to end the inning.

7. Renee walked to the deep end of the pool and <u>dived</u> in.

   The aircraft <u>dove</u> for the ground to avoid the attack.

8. We <u>dragged</u> the boat up the beach.

   Look what the cat <u>drug</u> in.

9. Coach Day <u>knit</u> together a winning team out of second-string players.

   My aunt <u>knitted</u> me a shirt for my birthday.

10. Ruth <u>lighted</u> the candles and set the table.

    A smile <u>lit</u> up her face.

TROUBLESOME VERBS: *LIE/LAY, RISE/RAISE, SIT/SET*

The forms of the verbs *lie* and *lay* are frequently confused; they have similar spellings and are close in meaning. *Lie* means "to recline, place oneself down, or to remain" and is intransitive (not followed by an object). *Lay* means "to put something down" and is transitive (must be followed by an object). Here are their principal forms:

	base	-s form	-ing form	-ed form	-en form
intransitive:	lie	lies	lying	lay	lain
transitive:	lay	lays	laying	laid	laid

As you can see, the word *lay* is both the -ed (past) form of *lie* and the base (present) form of *lay*. Even well-educated speakers have trouble choosing the correct forms of these two verbs in spontaneous speech, because the standard forms are so rarely heard. The most common errors occur with using *laid* for the past tense and past participle of *lie*:

*"The weary nurse laid down for a short nap."

*"She has laid down for a nap."

The standard forms, however, should always be used in edited writing:

The weary nurse lay down for a short nap

She has lain down for a nap.

Two other verb pairs—sit and set, and rise and raise—can cause some confusion because of their differing intransitive and transitive forms.

Rise is intransitive and irregular: *rise, rising, rose, risen.* It means "to get up" or "increase."

Raise is transitive and regular: *raise, raising, raised, raised.* It means "to lift something" or "bring up something."

Sit is intransitive and irregular: *sit, sitting, sat, sat.* It means "to be seated" or "be located."

Set is transitive and irregular: *set, setting, set, set.* It means "to put or place something."

Exercise 4.4
Using the Standard Verb Form

Directions: Decide if you need a transitive or intransitive verb to fill the blanks in the following paragraph. Choose the standard form from among these six verbs—*lie/lay, rise/raise, sit/set*—that accurately and correctly completes the meaning of each sentence.

     Our cat loves to _____ in the sun. Every morning after the sun _____, when I _____ the window shade, the cat jumps up and _____ on the window sill. Our dog, however, is a lazy creature who would rather _____ around on the rug all day and sleep. Yesterday he _____ there the entire day. Once in a while he _____ his head from the rug and looks around to see what the cat is doing. Sometimes my mother takes the cat outdoors and _____ her on the porch swing. She _____ there for hours.

Test Exercise 4.5

Identifying Sentence Patterns and Verb Components

Directions: In the parentheses after each sentence, identify its sentence pattern. On the line below, show the components of the verb. Your instructor may also ask you to diagram the sentences. [Answers are not given.]

Example:

Researchers have found no link between coffee consumption and heart disease. (VII)

_____Pres + have + -en + find_____

1. The federal government recently announced its new regulations for food labels. (____)

   _____

2. Some manufacturers were already using the new format. (____)

   _____

3. The old labels gave consumers very little information about fat content. (____)

   _____

4. Heart disease is the major cause of death in this country. (____)

   _____

5. Very high cholesterol levels may increase the risk of heart attacks. (____)

   _____

6. According to recent research, very low levels also pose a health hazard. (____)

   _____

7. My doctor has always considered nutrition the key to good health. (____)

   _____

8. Because of my low-sodium diet, potato chips taste extremely salty to me. (_____)

_____

9. The whole family will be eating more fresh vegetables now. (_____)

_____

10. Our nephew has been coming to dinner on Saturday nights. (_____)

_____

Chapter 5

Changing Sentence Focus

In Chapter 5 of *Understanding English Grammar*, you learned about three common ways of varying sentence patterns to change the focus of a sentence: the **passive voice**, the *there*-**transformation**, and **cleft sentences**. The exercises in this chapter will give you additional practice in understanding and using these focusing techniques.

THE PASSIVE VOICE

The verb-expansion rule represents the system for generating verbs in all of the sentence patterns. You can think of it as the "active" rule. The four transitive-verb patterns, however, have another version: the **passive voice**. We go through two main steps in transforming an active sentence to passive:

1. The direct object of the active is shifted to subject position.

2. *be* + *-en* is added to the verb formula.

Here, for example, is an active sentence:

> The students have eaten the pizza.

First, let's analyze the components of the verb, *have eaten*:

> **pres + have + -en + eat**

To transform the sentence into the passive voice, we add *be* + *-en*, just before the main verb:

> **pres + have + -en +** *be* **+** *-en* **+ eat**

The passive verb becomes *has been eaten*.

You'll notice that when we shift the direct object, *the pizza*, into subject position, the sentence no longer has a direct object:

> The pizza has been eaten.

We could add the original subject, or agent, to the passive by using a prepositional phrase (*by the students*), but often a passive sentence has no agent mentioned. The sentence is grammatical without it.

The resulting sentence,

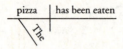

may look like Pattern VI—but don't be fooled: It's still Pattern VII. Remember that sentences are classified into patterns according to their verbs. Pattern VI is the class of intransitive verbs. *Has been eaten* is clearly not an intransitive verb. How do you know? Because it's passive, and only transitive verbs have a passive version. (And how can you recognize it as passive? Because it has a form of *be* as an auxiliary *not* followed by an *-ing* verb.)

You can also identify the voice of the sentence—whether active or passive—on the basis of meaning. Is the subject the actor, or agent—the "doer" of the action named by the verb? Or is the subject the passive receiver of the action? Think about the pizza. It's not doing anything; something's being done to it!

The indirect object of a Pattern VIII sentence can also become the subject of the passive version:

(active) The candidate granted <u>Tania</u> <u>an interview</u>.
ind obj   **dir obj**

(passive) Tania was granted an interview.

Notice that the direct object (*an interview*) remains in its slot after the verb.

If the direct object of a Pattern VIII sentence is used for the passive subject, the indirect object (if retained) is usually expressed in a prepositional phrase beginning with *to* or *for:*

An interview was granted to Tania.

Exercise 5.1
Transforming Active Sentences to Passive

Directions: In this exercise you will follow three steps in transforming the sentences into the passive voice:

Step 1: On the first line below the sentence, identify the components of the verb. Your answer will be in the form of a string, beginning with tense—present or past.

Step 2: Add be + *–en* to the components of the active verb.

Step 3: Then on the next line, write out the passive version of the sentence. Remember that the direct or indirect object will become the subject of the passive. In some cases you may wish to include the active subject (as the object of the preposition *by*); in others you may wish to drop it.

Example:

> You <u>will retain</u> all of the components of the active verb string.
>
> pres + will + retain; pres + will + be + -en + retain
>
> *Passive:* All of the components of the active verb string will be retained.

1. Sidney Rosenthal invented the indelible market in 1952.

    _____

    _____

2. He placed a felt tip on the end of a small bottle of permanent ink.

    _____

    _____

3. People have used Magic Markers for branding cattle, camouflaging fishing lines, and marking up buildings and subway cars.

    _____

    _____

4. The company sells more than half a billion markers each year.

_____

_____

5. The price of gasoline has altered our vacation plans for the summer.

_____

_____

6. The landscape center is installing a huge air-conditioning unit.

_____

_____

7. The new air-conditioning unit will regulate the humidity in the nurseries.

_____

_____

8. Every candidate for graduation must take a writing competency exam.

_____

_____

9. The prosecutor could have overlooked some important evidence.

_____

_____

10. The whole town is discussing Laura's strange disappearance.

_____

_____

CHANGING PASSIVE TO ACTIVE

To convert a passive sentence into an active one, begin by looking for these three elements:

1. *The agent or doer of the action expressed by the verb.* It's usually located in a *by* phrase. If an agent is not included in the passive sentence, then you'll have to create one. Remember, it will serve as the subject of the active sentence.

2. *The* be *auxiliary in the passive verb.* It's always the last auxiliary in the verb string and is always followed by the *-en* form of the main verb. You will delete this auxiliary and not include it in the active sentence.

3. *The subject of the passive sentence.* You will shift it to the object slot in the active sentence.

Let's take a look at a passive sentence and see how this analysis helps us to rewrite the sentence in active voice.

These lines were written by a famous poet.

- The agent of the action, "a famous poet," will become the subject of the active sentence.
- The passive auxiliary, "were," is in the past tense. Delete "were"; then change the main verb from "written" (the *-en* form) to "wrote" (the past tense).
- The passive subject, "These lines," goes in the direct object slot of the active sentence.

A famous poet wrote these lines. [*active version*]

Here are two more examples:

These lines are often quoted.

- There's no agent, so supply a noun phrase like "people" as the subject.
- Delete "are" (present tense) and use "quote" (present tense) for the verb.
- Move "these lines" to the direct object slot. (Put the adverb "often" wherever it fits.)

People often quote these lines. [*active version*].

These lines have been frequently quoted by politicians.

- "Politicians" becomes the subject.
- Delete "been" but keep "have"; the main verb remains the *-en* form ("quoted").

- Use "these lines" for the direct object; put the adverb "frequently" before the main verb or at the end of the sentence.

  Politicians have frequently quoted these lines. [*active version*]

  Politicians have quoted these lines frequently. [*active version*]

With a "give" verb the passive subject may shift to the indirect object slot in the active version:

  The author was offered a huge advance for his new novel. [*passive version*]

  A publisher offered the author a huge advance for his new novel. [*active version*]

Exercise 5.2

Changing Passive Sentences to Active

Directions: Change these passive sentences into active voice. Remember to locate the agent of the action, delete the passive *be*, and shift the passive subject to an object slot. If the agent of the action is not expressed in the passive sentence, you will have to supply a subject (such as *someone*) for the active sentence. Identify the sentence pattern of the active sentences that you produce.

Example:

Many lives have been saved by the discovery of insulin.

The discovery of insulin has saved many lives. (VII)

1. My wallet was turned in to the lost-and-found department.

2. Several ingredients were inadvertently omitted from the cheesecake receipe.

3. The country of Indonesia is made up of more than 17,000 islands.

4. My father has not been told about my brother's escapade in Spain.

5. Raoul's valuables are kept in a safe in his office.

6. Donations for the local food bank are being collected by the Boy Scouts.

7. Paula's credit card application was approved.

8. Our tests should be graded on the curve.

9. The president's economic plan is being called a failure by members of Congress.

10. Your suggestions will be given thoughtful consideration.

Exercise 5.3

Changing the Voice of Sentences

Directions:

   Step 1: In the parentheses after each sentence, identify the voice of the verb as active (A) or passive (P).

   Step 2: Rewrite the sentences, changing the active ones to passive and the passive to active. Again, remember that the only difference between the passive and active verb strings is the presence or absence of *be + -en.*

Example:

   Our company will give everyone a bonus at the end of the year. (A)

   Everyone will be given a bonus at the end of the year. (P)

1. In the Middle Ages monks copied thousands of manuscripts by hand. (_____)

   _____

   _____

2. The residents of Shady Pines are really enjoying their big screen TV. (_____)

   _____

   _____

3. The apartment was leased to us under false pretenses. (_____)

   _____

   _____

4. Contestants on *Jeopardy!* must phrase their answers in the form of a question. (_____)

   _____

   _____

5. Travel times between London and Paris have been considerably reduced by the Channel Tunnel. (_____)

_____

_____

6. The tunnel beneath the English Channel is called "The Chunnel." (_____)

_____

_____

7. The earthquake could be felt by people in three neighboring states. (_____)

_____

_____

8. These heavy socks will keep my feet warm in winter. (_____)

_____

_____

9. The fruit should be diced and soaked in brandy. (_____)

_____

_____

10. A little nonsense now and then is cherished by the wisest people. (_____)

_____

_____

THE *THERE* TRANSFORMATION

The *there* construction, like the passive voice, shifts the focus of a sentence by altering the word order. In this case, the unstressed *there*, known as an **expletive**, opens the sentence and is usually followed by a form of the verb *be*. This arrangement is sometimes called the "existential *there*" because it is used to state that something exists or simply *is*.

There is still time for a swim.

There were a lot of trucks on the road yesterday.

Handbooks for writers often warn that opening a sentence with *there* can create problems with subject-verb agreement and contribute to wordiness. But the *there* transformation is an effective way to refocus a sentence by postponing the subject. Other methods vary the information in a sentence by focusing on individual elements inside a clause, but the *there* transformation presents the whole sentence as new information.

In the following exercise you will examine a passage in which the author uses a series of *there* sentences to build up his description, moving through the scene to focus on certain details. The *there* constructions prepare the ground for the new items of information as they are added to the description.

Exercise 5.4
Exploring the Use of the *There* Transformation

Directions: The following is a passage from Chapter 3 of Ernest Hemingway's *For Whom the Bell Tolls*; it uses seven *there* transformations to describe a scene at a sentry box. The version below has been rewritten to eliminate those constructions. Your task is to restore the description to its original wording, including the seven *there* constructions.

(Hint: The third sentence is correct; it's the only sentence in the original that did not contain a *there* transformation.)

A worn, blackened leather wine bottle was on the wall of the sentry box, some newspapers were there, and no telephone. Of course a telephone could be on the side he could not see; but no wires running from the box were visible. A telephone line ran along the road and the wires were carried over the bridge. A charcoal brazier made from an old petrol tin with the top cut off and holes punched in it, which rested on two stones, was outside the sentry box; but it held no fire. Some fire-blackened empty tins were in the ashes under it.

CLEFT SENTENCES

A cleft sentence is one that is split (cleft) so as to put the focus on one part of it. In Chapter 5 of *Understanding English Grammar*, you learned that there are two ways of shifting focus with a cleft sentence: the *it*-cleft and the *what* cleft.

Exercise 5.5
Using Cleft Sentences

A. *Directions:* Rewrite each of the following sentences with an *it*-cleft to change the focus. Write two cleft versions, each one putting emphasis on a different part of the original sentence. You may prefer to use the passive voice in some of your rewrites.

Example:

Tom felt a sharp pain in his stomach.

It was Tom who felt a sharp pain in his stomach.

It was in his stomach that Tom felt a sharp pain.

1. The onions ruined the stew.

   _____

   _____

2. Fernando wore a white suit to the dance last night.

   _____

   _____

3. Ruth's father won $500 in an amateur photography contest.

   _____

   _____

4. Starr Jones criticized Barbara Walters for writing a tell-all memoir.

   _____

   _____

5. Myrtle's special marinated mushrooms added a gourmet touch to the salad.

_____

_____

6. The new technology of brain imaging is bringing hope to people suffering from Alzheimer's disease.

_____

_____

B. *Directions:* Use the *what*-cleft to shift the focus to one part of the sentence.

    Example: This version of the story illustrates the author's originality.

                    What this version of the story illustrates is the author's originality.

1. I want a good sleep.

_____

2. The defendant's consistent testimony convinced the jury.

_____

3. Hundreds of angry voters were protesting the candidate's position on the war.

_____

4. I disliked the movie's sophomoric humor.

_____

5. The encroachment of civilization on wilderness areas concerns a great many environmentalists.

_____

6. The voters want a fair election.

_____

Test Exercise 5.6

Identifying Shifts in Focus

Directions: In the parentheses, identify the pattern of the basic sentence underlying each of the following transformed sentences. On the line beneath the sentence, identify the structural shift in focus that the sentence has undergone: passive voice, there transformation, or cleft sentence. [Answers are not given.]

Example:

The students have been given their homework assignment. (VII)
_____Passive_____

1. There is always a traffic jam in the parking lot at noon. (_____)

   _____

2. The street in front of our house was resurfaced on Monday. (_____)

   _____

3. There were too many suspects in last night's episode of *CSI*. (_____)

   _____

4. What brings tourists to New England in October is the magnificent display of fall colors. (_____)

   _____

5. It was your stolen base in the ninth inning that set up the winning run. (_____)

   _____

6. There's no business like show business. (_____)

   _____

7. Several students from our dorm were questioned about the incident. (_____)

_____

8. It was my roommate who broke up the fight. (_____)

_____

9. What Maxine sent her mother for Christmas was a poinsettia. (_____)

_____

10. The food at that restaurant is often served too cold. (____)

_____

11. There appears on the screen an image of the planet Neptune. (_____)

_____

12. The team's new mascot was named Ruggers. (_____)

_____

Chapter 6

Modifiers of the Verb: Adverbials

Many of the sentences you have seen so far include **adverbials**—modifiers of the verb that add such information as time, place, reason, and manner. In Exercise 2.3 your task was to distinguish adverbial prepositional phrases from adjectivals, those that modify nouns. Here's the example from that exercise, with its three prepositional phrases:

> Many industries <u>from the United States</u> have built manufacturing plants
> <u>in Mexico</u> <u>in the last two years</u>.

The first is adjectival, modifying *industries*. You can test its function by substituting a pronoun for the subject of the sentence:

> <u>They</u> have built manufacturing plants….

The fact that the pronoun substitutes for the entire phrase, "Many industries from the United States," demonstrates that the "from" phrase modifies the noun.

The "in" prepositional phrases, however, are clearly adverbial, telling *where* and *when* about the verb. The last one is easy to test: It could open the sentence without changing the meaning:

> In the last two years they have built manufacturing plants in Mexico.

However, we probably wouldn't shift this particular "where" information:

> In Mexico in the last two years, many industries have built manufacturing plants.

The sentence is grammatical, but it doesn't sound quite as natural.

The movability test is not infallible. There are a number of adverbs and adverbial prepositional phrases that would not be idiomatic in the opening slot. However, if the prepositional phrase *can* be moved to the opening, it is clearly adverbial.

Exercise 6.1

Recognizing Adverbials

Directions: This exercise is similar to the one you did in Chapter 2 where you distinguished adverbial and adjectival prepositional phrases. Here, too, the sentences include both functions of the prepositional phrase. They also include adverbs, some of which are recognizable by the *-ly* endings (adverbs of manner, you'll recall, are derived by adding *-ly* to adjectives). Others you can identify by the kind of information they contribute to the sentence.

Underline the adverbial words and phrases. Draw an arrow from the underline to the verb being modified.

Examples:

The people across the hall often have noisy parties on the weekends.

Several friends are coming to my apartment on Saturday night for a party.

1. One wall of the study was filled with art works by the French impressionists.

2. How do people in the tropics live comfortably with such heat and humidity?

3. Northerners sometimes suffer from depression during the dark days of winter.

4. The decline in the financial markets probably happened because of uncertain news about interest rates.

5. The road to hell is often paved with good intentions.

6. According to recent estimates, almost 300 vertebrate species have become extinct during the past 300 years.

7. Several species are teetering precariously on the brink of extinction.

8. The students from Ms. Tingle's class walked single file down the corridor.

9. Detective Benson cautiously crept into the dark alley and quickly flattened herself against the wall.

10. In spite of my best efforts, I seldom do my physics experiments right the first time.

Your instructor may ask you to diagram the ten sentences from this exercise on separate paper. Identifying the pattern of each sentence will help you determine the basic shape of the diagram.

Exercise 6.2

Identifying and Diagramming Adverbials

Directions: In this exercise, you will encounter all five forms of adverbials that you studied in Chapter 6 of *Understanding English Grammar:* adverbs, prepositional phrases, noun phrases, verb phrases, and clauses. Underline each adverbial and identify its form.

Example:

<u>Last night</u> the wind was blowing <u>hard</u>.
   NP   adv

Using separate paper, diagram the ten sentences. Remember that all of the words and word groups that you identified as adverbal will be attached to a verb.

1. Theo will stay home on Saturday to prepare us a special dinner.

2. After my parents retire, they will move to a condo in Arizona.

3. I finally landed a part-time job as a lifeguard at the YMCA this summer.

4. Opportunities for full-time work are scarce in this economy.

5. At the time of the thunderstorm the family was quietly eating lunch on the patio.

6. At Mike's Halloween party, a ghostly face appeared in the window at midnight.

7. To get to work on time, I must get up at 4:30 a.m.

8. While you are in the kitchen, bring me some extra cream for my coffee.

9. To receive a refund, you must sign a release form before you purchase this product.

10. Life would be happier if we could be born at the age of eighty and gradually approach eighteen. [Mark Twain]

Exercise 6.3
Combining Sentences with Adverbial Clauses

Directions: Combine each of the following pairs of sentences into a single sentence by reducing one of the original sentences to an adverbial clause. As you know, adverbial clauses begin with **subordinating conjunctions**, words that establish the relationship between clauses. Here is a list of the most frequently used subordinators:

> *To indicate time:* before, after, as, as soon as, when, whenever, until, once
>
> *To indicate cause:* because, since
>
> *To indicate purpose:* in order that, so that
>
> *To indicate condition:* if, provided that, once
>
> *To indicate place:* where, wherever
>
> *To indicate concession:* though, although, even though, except that

Put a comma after an adverbial clause that comes at the beginning of a sentence. When an adverbial clause follows an independent clause, no comma is needed, unless the subordinator expresses a contrast.

Examples:

> Our family wanted to see Carlsbad Caverns.
>
> We drove to New Mexico last summer.
>
> We drove to New Mexico last summer because our family wanted to see
>
> Carlsbad Caverns.
>
> We arrived early in the morning.
>
> We still had to wait in line for an hour.
>
> Although we arrived early in the morning, we still had to wait in line for an hour.

1. We waited for the tour to start.
   My sister and I read the brochure about stalactites and stalagmites.

   _____

   _____

2. These amazing formations look like artistic sculptures.
   They have been formed naturally by dripping groundwater.

   _____

   _____

3. We wanted to see these natural wonders with our own eyes.
   We would have to wait for the tour to start.

   _____

   _____

4. The tour finally started.
   It was certainly worth the wait.

   _____

   _____

5. We hiked along a trail more than 700 feet underground.
   We came to the largest subterranean chamber in the world.

   _____

   _____

6. We looked around the enormous room.
   We saw stalactites and stalagmites everywhere.

   _____

   _____

Exercise 6.4

Prepositional and Infinitive Phrases

Directions: The purpose of this exercise is to help you distinguish between prepositional phrases with *to* and adverbial infinitive phrases, which also begin with *to*. Underline each *to* phrase; identify each as *prepositional* (prep) or *infinitive* (inf); then give its function in the sentence. The infinitive phrases in this exercise will be adverbial (adv); the prepositional phrases will be either adjectival (adj) or adverbial (adv). Remember that the difference between the two kinds of *to* phrases is the form of the word group that follows: Infinitive phrases are verb phrases; a noun phrase will follow the preposition *to* as its object.

Example:

      My roommate went <u>to the store</u> <u>to get some snacks</u>.
                prep—adv   inf—adv

1. To keep its audiences happy, the Art Theater changes its films every week.

2. Don't cut off your nose to spite your face.

3. Jacqueline transferred to a college in Michigan to be near her family.

4. She applied to the registrar to get on the transfer list.

5. To get a better view we climbed to the top of the monument.

6. The Sixth Amendment to the Constitution guarantees all citizens the right to a speedy and public trail.

7. We moved up three rows to get closer to the stage.

8. To get detailed directions for our trip to Mt. Hood, Lena logged on to the Internet.

9. Walter and Renee went to the computer show to check out the new laptops.

10. Do not use a hatchet to remove a fly from a friend's forehead. [Chinese proverb]

Exercise 6.5

Composing with Adverbials

A. *Directions:* Finish these sentences, adding adverbials in the positions shown.

Example:

> [prep ph] the weather turned cold [adv].
>
> *Rewrite:* <u>On Monday the weather turned cold suddenly.</u>

1. [inf ph] the neighborhood children decided to start a lawn-mowing service [prep ph].

    _____

2. [prep ph] the children earned more money than they expected [clause].

    _____

3. [adv] [prep ph] the president announced a new economic plan [inf ph].

    _____

4. [clause] the Congress [adv] agreed that the new plan had merit.

    _____

5. [prep ph] the students were angry [clause].

    _____

6. The fans were ecstatic [NP] [clause].

    _____

B. *Directions:* Follow the instructions for writing sentences that include adverbials. Remember that adverbial clauses and infinitives themselves contain verbs, so those two adverbial word groups can include other adverbials.

1. Write a sentence about one of your classes that includes an adverbial clause.

   _____

   _____

2. Write a sentence about a holiday that includes an adverb of manner. Underline the adverb.

   _____

   _____

3. Write a sentence about your plans for the future that includes two adverbial prepositional phrases. Underline them.

   _____

   _____

4. Write a sentence about your favorite sport that includes an adverbial noun phrase. Underline the adverbial.

   _____

   _____

5. Write a sentence about your neighborhood that includes both an adverbial infinitive and an adverbial clause. Underline and label the two adverbials.

   _____

   _____

6. Write a sentence about last weekend that includes both an adverbial prepositional phrase and an adjectival prepositional phrase. Underline and label the two.

   _____

   _____

Test Exercise 6.6
Identifying Form and Function

Directions: On the lines following the passage, identify each of the underlined words and word groups according to both its form and function. *Form* refers to word categories (noun, verb, preposition, determiner, etc.), names of phrases (prepositional phrase, noun phrase, infinitive phrase), and clauses (adverbial clause). *Function* refers to the specific role the word or word group plays in the sentence: subject, direct object, modifier of *play*, etc. You'll find it helpful to picture the sentence on a diagram to figure out the function of the underlined element. [Answers are not given.]

Examples:	*Form*	*Function*
He drove <u>his car</u> around the track.	noun ph	direct object
He drove the car <u>around the track</u>.	prep ph	modifier of "drove"

Born in Kingston, England, in 1830, Eadweard Muybridge immigrated <u>to</u>

<u>California</u> in the 1850s. He took <u>up</u> photography and <u>quickly</u> became one of the first
   1   2   3

internationally known photographers. <u>Between 1867 and 1872</u>, he took more than 2,000
                                     4

photographs, many of them views <u>of the Yosemite Valley</u>. <u>Although he gained fame</u>
                               5   6

<u>for his landscape and architectural photos</u>, Muybridge <u>also</u> designed <u>a new camera</u>
                                  7   8

that could take a picture <u>in one-thousandth of a second</u>. <u>To test his improvement</u>, he set
                           9   10

up 24 cameras <u>along a racetrack</u> with tripwires to pull the shutters. <u>With those cameras</u>,
               11   12

he took a series of pictures <u>of a horse galloping</u>, which showed for <u>the first time</u> that all
                        13   14

four of a horse's hooves will <u>sometimes</u> be off the ground <u>at the same time</u>.
                        15   16

	Form	**Function**
1.	_____	_____
2.	_____	_____
3.	_____	_____
4.	_____	_____
5.	_____	_____
6.	_____	_____
7.	_____	_____
8.	_____	_____
9.	_____	_____
10.	_____	_____
11.	_____	_____
12.	_____	_____
13.	_____	_____
14.	_____	_____
15.	_____	_____
16.	_____	_____

Chapter 7

Modifiers of the Noun: Adjectivals

The **noun phrase** is the most common word group in English, having many roles to play and many slots to fill in our sentences. In fact, the sentence you just read contains six:

the noun phrase

many roles to play

the most common word group in English

many slots to fill

English

our sentences

You may not have counted the single word *English* as a noun phrase, but, as you learned in Chapter 2 of *Understanding English Grammar*, some noun phrases do consist of only the headword.

This chapter, which covers adjectivals, or noun modifiers, is actually about noun phrases. It describes the noun **headword**—the common element in all noun phrases—along with all of the modifiers that fill the slots before and after the headword.

THE DETERMINER

The opening slot of the noun phrase is filled by a **determiner**, the most common of which are the **articles**, *a(n)* and *the*. The possessives are another important group of determiners: **possessive pronouns** (*my, his, her, its, their, your*), **possessive nouns** (*Pam's*), and **possessive noun phrases** (*the neighbors'* yard, *my little sister's* bicycle). Two other classes of pronouns can also function as determiners: the **indefinite pronouns** (*several, many,* etc.) and the four demonstrative pronouns (*this, that, these,* and *those*). **Numbers** also act as determiners. The five determiners in the opening sentence of this chapter include two uses of the definite article (*the*), two uses of an indefinite pronoun (*many*), and a possessive pronoun (*our*).

The determiner, then, signals the beginning of a noun phrase. In the first exercise you will review determiners and headwords. Next you will study the system of modifiers that fill the slots before and after the headword.

Copyright © 2009 by Pearson Education, Inc., Publishing as Longman

81

Exercise 7.1

Identifying Determiners and Noun Phrases

Directions. In the following sentences, circle the headword of each noun phrase; underline the determiner, if there is one, and label its word class.

Example:

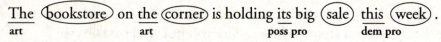

The <u>book</u>store on the corner is holding its big sale this week.
art   art   poss pro   dem pro

1. In my opinion, the candidate's rash remarks have raised serious questions for many voters.

2. Several students dropped out of my botany class after the midterm exam.

3. Our exams in that class would have challenged Luther Burbank.

4. Many winners of this year's Oscars were complete surprises.

5. Few substitute teachers in the public schools can serve a full year without any problems.

6. My cousin's second husband came from Ireland.

7. Their oldest son works in his uncle's office in Dublin.

8. The hockey team scored three goals in the first period of last night's game.

9. Our team will probably win the division championship this year.

10. Clarice made those beautiful quilts out of scraps from her family's old clothes.

THE PREPOSITIONAL PHRASE

As you know from Chapter 6, one of the most common adverbial word groups is the prepositional phrase. It is also a common adjectival word group. Sometimes it's tricky to figure out which function a prepositional phrase is performing. For example, consider the following sentence:

> They discussed their problem with the teacher.

Without more information, we don't know if the prepositional phrase modifies *discussed* or *problem.* In this case the sentence is ambiguous.

One important difference between the two functions is the movability of the adverbial and the nonmovability of the adjectival: An adjectival prepositional phrase is always there in the noun phrase, most of the time directly following the noun headword (sometimes in the subject complement slot). But most adverbial prepositional phrases are movable: Many can either begin or end the sentence without a change in meaning. For example, in this sentence,

> We went to the Fiesta Bowl <u>on New Year's Day.</u>

the closing prepositional phrase could open the sentence with no change in meaning:

> <u>On New Year's Day</u> we went to the Fiesta Bowl.

That movability indicates that the prepositional phrase is adverbial; it is not a modifier of *Fiesta Bowl.* In the case of adverbials, we also have meaning to help us. When the phrase tells *when*, as in our example, its purpose is clearly adverbial.

An adjectival phrase, however, will identify the noun it modifies, telling *which one:*

> Their problem with the teacher is serious.

Which problem? The one with the teacher.

Remember, too, that an adjectival phrase can be embedded in an adverbial phrase—that is, an adjectival phrase can modify the object of an adverbial phrase:

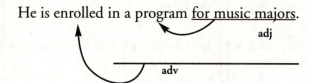

Exercise 7.2

Identifying and Diagramming Prepositional Phrases

Directions: Underline the prepositional phrases in the following sentences and identify them as either adjectival (adj) or adverbial (adv). Then, on separate paper, diagram the sentences.

Example:

My uncle <u>from Milwaukee</u> is moving <u>to Arizona</u> <u>for his health</u>.
              adj   adv   adv

1. Several symphony orchestras in the United States have canceled their contracts with highly paid soloists because of financial difficulties.

2. The neighbors down the street are having a party for all the children on the block.

3. According to the National Institutes of Health, fifteen million Americans suffer from carpal tunnel syndrome.

4. Our family stayed at a ski lodge for a whole week during the winter break.

5. You must see the beautiful flowering shrubs around the courthouse square.

6. Regular consumption of garlic can lower cholesterol in some people.

7. Maxine found the key to the door and put it in the lock.

8. The teachers in the local school district have been picketing for two months.

9. The contestant with the highest score will win a trip to Fiji.

10. If you leave the smallest corner of your mind vacant for a moment, other people's opinions will rush in from all quarters. [Mark Twain]

THE ADJECTIVAL CLAUSE

The **adjectival,** or **relative, clause** occupies the last slot in the noun phrase. Often, of course, the clause is the only postheadword modifier; but in those sentences where there are others, the clause will be the last in line:

> The people in line who are buying tickets for the concert will probably have to wait for several hours.

As you learned in Chapter 7 of *Understanding English Grammar,* adjectival clauses are introduced by **relative pronouns** or **relative adverbs**. For the most part, those relatives are the same words that in Chapter 3 you learned to identify as interrogatives. When they introduce adjectival clauses, words such as *who* and *which* and *why* and *where* are not asking questions or suggesting them; they are relating a clause to a noun as a modifier:

> My biology professor, who does research on frogs, worries because some species are becoming extinct.

The relative pronoun renames the noun headword; that is, the noun being modified is the antecedent of the relative pronoun. In the preceding example, the antecedent of *who* is "my biology professor." Relative adverbs introduce clauses that modify certain kinds of nouns: *where* clauses modify nouns of place (such as *town*); *when* clauses modify nouns of time; *why* clauses modify the noun *reason*.

> The town where I was born goes to sleep at 8:00 P.M.

One of the most common of the relative clause introducers is the relative pronoun *that:*

> The flavor that I prefer is pistachio nut.

Relative pronouns always perform a grammatical function in the clauses they introduce. In the earlier *who* clause, *who* is the subject; in the *that* clause, *that* is the direct object.

That can also serve as the subject of its clause:

> The flavor that sells best is vanilla.

When *that* is the direct object in its clause, it may be dropped:

> The flavor I prefer is pistachio nut.

You can still recognize the clause because it has a subject and verb: *I prefer.*

PUNCTUATING ADJECTIVAL CLAUSES

The way an adjectival clause relates to the noun it modifies determines the punctuation. An adjectival clause that is not required for identifying, or defining, the noun is set off with commas:

> Hawthorne Road, which runs past our house, is being repaved.

> Julia Losa, who lives at the end of Hawthorne Road, won the lottery.

The clauses—*which runs past our house* and *who lives at the end of Hawthorne Road*—give extra information that is not needed to define Hawthorne Road or Julia Losa; they simply comment on the nouns they modify.

An adjectival clause that is needed to identify the noun it modifies is not set off with commas:

> The road that runs past our house is being repaved.

> The woman who lives at the end of Hawthorne Road won the lottery.

The clauses—*that runs past our house* and *who lives at the end of Hawthorne Road*—supply the information that is necessary to identify "the road" and "the woman." In other words, they identify the referents of the nouns they modify. If these clauses were removed, the reader would no longer know which road is being repaved or which woman won the lottery. Such necessary clauses are written without commas.

Exercise 7.3

Identifying and Punctuating Adjectival Clauses

Directions: In the following sentences, underline the adjectival (relative) clauses. Put in commas if they are needed.

Example:

> Pasta, <u>which consists of flour and water and often eggs</u>, probably originated in the Middle East in the fifth century.

1. The familiar story that Marco Polo brought pasta back from China is just a legend.

2. Most Italians still cling to this legend which is not found in Polo's account of his travels.

3. The dried noodle-like product the Arabs introduced to Sicily in the eighth century is most likely the origin of dried pasta.

4. The best pasta is made with semolina flour which comes from hard durum wheat.

5. Italians traditionally cook their pasta *al dente* which is Italian for "to the tooth" and means "not too soft."

6. In other countries dry pasta is fequently made from common types of flour, such as farina which yields a softer product and cannot be cooked *al dente.*

7. The many ingredients that are added to pasta dough include cheese, spices, and even squid ink.

8. There was a time when all pasta was hand-rolled.

9. Today pasta is more commonly made with special machines, such as extrusion tools that force ingredients through holes in a copper plate.

10. Lamination tools squeeze ingredients through rollers into sheets of a particular thickness which are not cut by slitters.

11. Dried pastas which often have ridges or bumps are designed to grab and hold sauces.

12. American colonists first imported pasta from the English who had discovered it on their travels to Italy.

13. Italians eat over sixty pounds of pasta per person, per year, easily beating Americans who eat about twenty pounds per person annually.

14. The pasta dishes Americans eat most are spaghetti, macaroni, and ravioli.

For discussion: Look at the way you punctuated the *that* and *which* clauses. Is there a difference? Can you state a general rule that may apply?

THE PARTICIPIAL PHRASE

Another postheadword slot in the noun phrase is the **participial phrase**, an *-ing* or *-en* verb with all of its complements and modifiers. Unlike the adjectival prepositional phrase, the participial phrase is sometimes movable. We can think of the slot following the headword as the "home base" of the participial phrase, but when the participle modifies the subject, it can also open or close the sentence.

> The Boy Scouts, *carrying all their supplies on their backs,* finally reached their campsite on the mountaintop.

> *Carrying all their supplies on their backs,* the Boy Scouts finally reached their campsite on the mountaintop.

> The Boy Scouts finally reached their campsite on the mountaintop, *carrying all their supplies on their backs.*

The important feature to notice is that the noun being modified—in this case "Boy Scouts"—is the subject of the participle. A participle modifies its own subject. As you read in Chapter 7 of *Understanding English Grammar,* the participial phrase is, essentially, a reduced adjectival clause:

> The Boy Scouts, ~~who were~~ carrying all their supplies on their backs, finally....

We should note too that the diagram of the sentence always shows the participle attached to its subject as part of the noun phrase. In the case of this sentence, all three versions will be diagrammed the same:

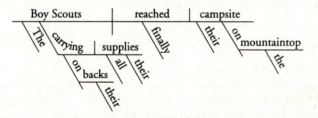

Note: In the diagram of the second version, "Carrying" will be capitalized.

Exercise 7.4

Practicing with Participles

Directions: Rewrite each of the following pairs of sentences as a single sentence, turning one of the two predicates into a participial phrase. Items 9 and 10 have three sentences; turn two of them into participial phrases. Remember that you have a choice in placing the participle. And in some cases you also have a choice as to which sentence will be the main clause and which one the participle.

Example:

The sailboat glided across the bay.
The sailboat looked majestic.

Rewrites: The sailboat gliding across the bay looked majestic.

or

Looking majestic, the sailboat glided across the bay.

or

Gliding across the bay, the sailboat looked majestic.

(Note: In some cases you may have to change the auxiliaries.)

1. The wind blew hard from the east.

   The wind damaged the maple trees in our front yard.

   _____

   _____

2. Ms. Ruggles was angered by the impertinence of the headwaiter.
   Ms. Ruggles turned and stalked out of the restaurant.

   _____

   _____

3. The shortstop leaped high in the air.
   The shortstop speared the line drive that would have won the game.

   _____

   _____

4. *The Scarlet Letter* was written in 1850.
   It tells the story of Hester Prynne.

   _____

   _____

5. Hester was shunned by the community.
   She bravely endured her shame and loneliness.

   _____

   _____

6. A man was standing in the hotel window.
   Nobody could identify the man.

   _____

   _____

7. The two boys were fascinated by the skills of the weaver.
   The two boys sat and watched the weaver's flying fingers for hours.

   _____

   _____

8. Barrow, Alaska, is located on the Arctic Circle.
   It is closer to the North Pole than to any other U.S. city.

   _____

   _____

9. Jean squinted hard at the note.
   Jean read the note in the dim light.
   The light came through the dirty window.

   _____

   _____

   _____

10. The dog heard the far-off thunder.
    He crept under the couch.
    He lay shivering with fright.

   _____

   _____

   _____

Exercise 7.5

Identifying and Diagramming Postnoun Modifiers

Directions: Underline all the postnoun modifiers in the following sentences. Label their form by writing one of these abbreviations below them: prep ph (for adjectival prepositional phrases), part ph (for participial phrases), inf (for adjectival infinitive) and adj cl (for adjectival clauses).

Example: The teenager <u>who lives across the street</u> rakes the leaves <u>in our yard</u> for a
                              adj cl   prep ph
reasonable price.

1. The first human who hurled an insult instead of a stone was the founder of

   civilization. [Sigmund Freud]

2. The thing generally raised on city land is taxes. [C. D. Warner]

3. The chief obstacle to the progress of the human race is the human race.

   [Don Marquis]

4. The good you do isn't always good for you.

5. A man gazing at the stars is proverbially at the mercy of the puddles in the road.

   [Alexander Smith]

6. He has the gall of a shoplifter returning an item for a refund.

7. The contestant with the most stamina has the best chance to win.

8. We should distrust any enterprise that requires new clothes.

   [Henry David Thoreu]

9. Progress is made by lazy people looking for an easier way to do things.

   [Robert Heinlein]

10. The players complaining loudest are the ones with the least talent.

11. He has all the virtues I dislike and none of the vices I admire.

    [Winston Churchill]

12. The 132 islands in the Hawaiian chain, which reaches across 1,600 miles of

    ocean, are actually the tops of volcanic mountains that erupted 25

    million years ago.

Now diagram these sentences on separate paper. In preparation for that job, draw lines to show the boundaries of the sentence slots and identify the sentence patterns.

Exercise 7.6
Revising Adjectival Clauses

Directions: The following sentences include adjectival clauses as modifiers in some of the noun phrases. Revise the sentences by reducing the adjectival clauses to verb phrases (participial phrases), prepositional phrases, noun phrases, or adjective phrases—if you can do so without losing information. Write your answers on the lines provided or on separate paper.

Example:

My neighbor *who lives across the street* raked my yard last week.

Rewrite: My neighbor across the street raked my yard last week.

1. The safe that contained the firm's important documents appears to have been stolen.

   _____

   _____

2. The children who are playing in the street don't see the car that is speeding toward them.

   _____

   _____

3. The thought that bothers him most involves a choice that's difficult.

   _____

   _____

4. According to some people, the Loch Ness monster, who is known as Nessie, may have some relatives who live in the lakes and coastal waters of British Columbia.

   _____

   _____

5. People who are interested in becoming astronauts should study science or engineering when they are in college.

_____

_____

6. The student who has sold the most raffle tickets will receive a free video game.

_____

_____

7. According to researchers who work at the Boston University School of Medicine, men who are bald have an increased risk of heart attack.

_____

_____

8. The International Date Line is an imaginary line that is fixed at 180° longitude, which is the location on earth that is exactly opposite Greenwich, England.

_____

_____

9. Cass looked at the clock, which was ticking slowly, and hoped for the lecture to end.

_____

_____

10. Children who are left-handed have more accidents than those who are right-handed, according to pediatricians who conducted a study at the Arkansas Children's Hospital.

_____

_____

DANGLING MODIFIERS

As you learned in Chapter 7 of *Understanding English Grammar*, readers assume that introductory participial and infinitive phrases will have the same subject as the subject of the main sentence. If that is not the case, the modifier "dangles":

> Staring in disbelief, the car jumped the curb and crashed into a mailbox.

> [Who was staring? Not the car.]

> To maintain a C average, a tutor meets with Tiffany three times a week.

> [Tiffany, not the tutor, wants a C average.]

You can usually revise dangling modifiers in one of two ways, depending on what you want to emphasize in the sentence:

- Make the subject of the main clause the same as the subject of the participle or infinitive:

    > Staring in disbelief, I watched the car jump the curb and crash into a mailbox.
    > To maintain a C average, Tiffany meets with a tutor three times a week.

- Rewrite the dangling modifier as a clause with its own subject and verb:

    > As I stared in disbelief, the car jumped the curb and crashed into a mailbox.
    > Because Tiffany wants to maintain a C average, her tutor has to meet with her three times a week.

Exercise 7.7

Revising Dangling Modifiers

Directions: Rewrite the following sentences to eliminate any dangling modifiers. Some sentences can be revised in more than one way.

1. Campaigning in 1960 as an exemplar of "vigor," John Kennedy's health often forced him to spend half the day in bed.

2. Growing up poor in rural Kansas, summers always meant extra chores, a day job, and little time for a vacation.

3. To fix the problems with the draft of your essay, a trip to the writing center is recommended.

4. Given some direction and encouragement, life for this gifted but troubled teen might have turned out different.

5. Excited by the pounding music, there was nothing to do but join the crowd on the dance floor.

6. Getting up early, the house seemed unusually quiet to me.

7. Not completely finished with the test, the proctor told the students to put their pencils down anyway.

8. Outdated and completely unworkable, the coaches decided to revise the team's code of conduct.

9. Hearing about Alanis Morrisette's newly released album, my first thought was "Why?"

10. Praised by critics and parents alike, the lack of success with older audiences led to the film's quick disappearance from theaters.

MODIFIER PLACEMENT

You can ensure the correct interpretation of your sentences by paying close attention to where you place your modifiers. Consider how the meaning changes in these two sentences when the adverbial NP is shifted to a different position:

<u>Several times</u> the teacher told us to proofread our papers.

The teacher told us to proofread our papers <u>several times</u>.

A carelessly placed modifier can badly skew the meaning of a sentence:

DARE is sponsoring a series on drugs for local college students.

DARE is not in the business of acquainting college students with drugs to use. The meaning is clearer this way:

DARE is sponsoring a series for local college students on the dangers of drug use.

Putting the adjectival phrase next to the noun *series* illustrates the general rule about where to place a modifier: **as close as possible to the word it modifiers.**

Exercise 7.8

Revising Misplaced Modifiers

Directions: Rewrite the following sentences to eliminate problems with modifier placement.

1. In our neighborhood all dogs must be accompanied by an adult on a leash.

2. A Reno man encountered a range cow on the road, traveling by auto with his wife.

3. Abraham Lincoln wrote the Gettysburg Address while traveling from Washington to Gettysburg on the back of an envelope.

4. The student orchestra played far better than could be expected under the direction of Mr. Ducloux.

5. High cirrus clouds appeared as I approached the coastal ridgeline, whipping across the moon like horsetails.

6. At the end of the party, the hostess gave balloons to all the children in the shape of fantastic animals.

7. No matter how formulaic and sappy, few of us can forget our favorite teen movies.

8. According to the cohabitation policy, students cannot visit the dormitories of students who are of a different gender after one o'clock in the morning.

9. A memorial service will be held next Wednesday evening for Maud Hawkins, who died last week, at the request of her family.

10. Former hostage Terry Anderson will talk about his five years of confinement in Beirut with Barbara Walters in a special segment of *20/20*.

Test Exercise 7.9
Form and Function

Directions: On the lines following the passage, identify each of the underlined elements according to both its form and its function. Remember that *form* refers to word categories (noun, verb, preposition, etc.), names of phrases (prepositional phrase, noun phrase, infinitive phrase, participial phrase, etc.), and clauses (adverbial clause, adjectival [relative]clause). *Function* refers to the specific role the word or word group plays in the sentence: subject, direct object, modifier of *play,* etc. You'll find it helpful to picture the sentence on a diagram to figure out the function of the underlined item. [Answers are not given.]

The Navajo Code Talkers took part in every assault <u>that the U. S. Marines</u> [1]

<u>conducted in World War II.</u> They transmitted messages <u>by telephone and radio</u> in their [2]

native language—a code <u>the Japanese never broke.</u> Navajo answered the <u>military</u> [3] [4]

requirement <u>for an undecipherable code</u> because it had never been written down, [5]

<u>making it unintelligible without Navajo help.</u> In 1942, twenty-nine Navajos were recruited [6]

<u>to create the code.</u> They developed a dictionary <u>of words</u> for military terms, <u>which they</u> [7] [8]

<u>memorized during training.</u> <u>When a Code Talker completed training</u>, he was sent to a [9] [10]

Marine unit <u>deployed in the Pacific theater.</u> The original group became <u>an elite corps of</u> [11]

<u>425 Navajo Code Talkers.</u> Navajo remained potentially <u>valuable</u> even after the war. [12] [13]

In 1968 America <u>finally</u> learned of the extraordinary contribution <u>that a handful of Native</u> [14] [15]

<u>Americans had made to the war effort.</u>

Form Function

1. _____   _____

2. _____   _____

3. _____   _____

4. _____   _____

5. _____   _____

6. _____   _____

7. _____   _____

8. _____   _____

9. _____   _____

10. _____   _____

11. _____   _____

12. _____   _____

13. _____   _____

14. _____   _____

15. _____   _____

Chapter 8

The Noun Phrase Slots: Nominals

In Chapter 8 of *Understanding English Grammar* you learned the word **nominal**, the term that refers to the functions that noun phrases carry out. As you know, there are many specific nominal functions: Subject, subject complement, direct object, indirect object, and object complement are the NP slots in the sentence-pattern formulas. Another common nominal function is that of object of the preposition. The word *nominal,* then, is the general term for the function; these other words—subject, direct object, and so on—name the specific nominal functions.

The most common unit, or form, that functions as a nominal, as you know, is the noun phrase (NP). Except for pronouns, all of the nominals in previous exercises in this book have been noun phrases. The first exercise in this chapter will help you to review both the form and functions of NPs.

Name _____

Exercise 8.1

Composing and Using Noun Phrases

Directions: Generate noun phrases that conform to the following patterns; then for each NP write a sentence in which you use it as directed.

Example:

det + adj + N + prep phrase (use as object of a preposition)

my new friend from Des Moines

I talked to my new friend from Des Moines.

1. det + n + N + prep phrase (use as subject)

_____

_____

2. det + adj + N + part phrase (use as direct object)

_____

_____

3. det + N + part phrase (use as subject complement)

_____

_____

4. det + N + part phrase + clause (use as subject)

_____

_____

5. det + adj + N + clause (use as indirect object)

_____

_____

6. det + adj + n + N (use as direct object)

_____

_____

7. det + N + part phrase (use as object of preposition)

_____

_____

8. det + N + clause (use as object complement)

_____

_____

9. det + part + N + prep phrase   (use as subject complement)

_____

_____

APPOSITIVES

Another specific nominal function is the appositive, a structure that adds information by renaming another nominal. Usually a noun phrase in form, an appositive can be thought of as a nominal companion, with features of both a nominal and an adjectival. It renames another noun phrase or other nominal and can often substitute for that nominal, but as part of an NP, it adds information as adjectivals do.

> My large car, <u>an eight-cylinder model</u>, uses a lot of gas.

> My sister's car, <u>a Japanese import</u>, is inexpensive to drive.

Here the appositives give more details about the noun *car*.

Sometimes an appositive that renames the subject can be placed at the beginning of a sentence:

> <u>A Japanese import</u>, my sister's car is inexpensive to drive.

Exercise 8.2
Using Appositives

Directions: In this exercise you will practice adding appositives to one of the noun phrase slots by combining sentences. In each of the following sets of sentences, the second adds a detail about one of the noun phrases in the first. Your job is to turn that detail into an appositive. Write your answers on the lines provided or on separate paper. [Note that in Sentence 10 there are two details to turn into appositives.]

Example:

> Aunt Rachel loves her job. She's a butcher at Safeway.
>
> *Rewrite:* Aunt Rachel, a butcher at Safeway, loves her job.

1. Representative Henry Waxman chairs the House Committee on Oversight and Government Reform. Waxman is a Democrat from California.

    _____

    _____

2. The deepest part of the ocean is located in the Western Pacific near the island of Guam. It is the Marianas Trench.

    _____

    _____

3. Richard Jordan Gatling invented the world's first successful machine gun. He was a self-taught inventor from Indiana.

_____

_____

4. His weapon could mow down rows of soldiers like so many stalks of wheat. It was called the Gatling gun.

_____

_____

5. Gatling refused to sell his gun to the Confederacy. He was the son of a slaveholder.

_____

_____

6. Chinua Achebe has been called "the patriach of the African novel." He is a Nigerian novelist.

_____

_____

7. Achebe's masterpiece is one of the first works of fiction to present village life from an African perspective. It's entitled *Things Fall Apart*.

_____

_____

8. My brother's name is Rafael. He is a terrific soccer player.

_____

_____

9. You lack the one ability needed for this job. That is a commitment to the task at hand.

_____

_____

10. Duncan Hines began his career by writing *Adventures in Good Eating*. He was one of America's most successful food manufacturers. His book was a traveler's guide to America's best restaurants.

_____

_____

FORMS OF NOMINALS

In Chapter 8 of *Understanding English Grammar* you saw that forms other than noun phrases can still fill the nominal slots. These include verb phrases and clauses.

> <u>Riding a bicycle</u> is terrific exercise.

> Mike is planning <u>to buy a new bike</u>.

> I wonder <u>who owns this mountain bike</u>.

In the first example an *-ing* verb phrase, a gerund phrase, fills the subject slot; in the second an infinitive phrase occupies the direct object position; and in the third a nominal clause is the direct object.

NOMINAL VERB PHRASES

Nominal verb phrases come in two forms, the gerund and the infinitive, as illustrated by the earlier examples:

> <u>Riding a bike</u> is terrific exercise. [gerund]

> Mike is planning <u>to buy a new bike</u>. [infinitive]

The diagrams will help you recognize both of the verb phrases—*riding a bike* and *to buy a new bike*—as Pattern VII:

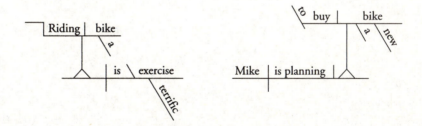

Here are some further examples of gerund phrases and infinitive phrases that fill the subject or direct object slots in sentences:

subject: <u>Missing that turn on the highway</u> has made us late.

<u>To get home by midnight</u> will now be impossible.

direct object: I wanted <u>to lose thirty pounds</u>.

I tried <u>skipping every other meal</u>.

But we can also use these verb phrases in other nominal slots:

subject complement: Our toughest job is <u>finding qualified candidates</u>.

Our plan is <u>to advertise in the school newspaper</u>.

object of a preposition: He cannot discipline the children without <u>losing his temper</u>.

Although gerunds and infinitives function as nouns, they retain their internal structure as verb phrases. That means they may include objects and complements and adverbial modifiers. In the sentences above, "that turn on the highway," "thirty pounds," "every other meal," "qualified candidates," and "his temper" are NPs that fill the direct object slots within the nominal verb phrases; and "home," "by midnight," and "in the school newspaper" are adverbial phrases that modify the gerund or infinitive.

Exercise 8.3

Understanding Nominal Verb Phrases

Directions: This exercise has two steps:

Step 1: Reduce the predicate in each of the following sentences into (1) an *-ing* phrase and (2) an infinitive phrase.

Example:

We mowed the lawn for the neighbors.

-ing: mowing the lawn for the neighbors

_____

infinitive: to mow the lawn for the neighbors

_____

1. Our candidate won the election in a landslide.

_____

_____

2. We went to the movies.

_____

_____

3. Shelley lost her keys.

_____

_____

4. Terry is a good teacher.

_____

_____

5. I made too many mistakes on this biology homework.

_____

_____

6. Stacie painted her bedroom lavender.

_____

_____

7. The instructor gave the students an extra assignment.

   _____

   _____

8. Pat felt upset about the homework.

   _____

   _____

Step 2: Write eight sentences, including as a nominal either the *-ing* phrase or the infinitive phase you wrote in Step 1.

Example:

> We decided to mow the lawn for the neighbors.
>
> > or
>
> Mowing the lawn for the neighbors was a good idea.

1. _____

   _____

2. _____

   _____

3. _____

   _____

4. _____

   _____

5. _____

   _____

6. _____

   _____

7. _____

   _____

8. _____

   _____

Exercise 8.4

Understanding *To*-Phrases

Directions: You may recall Exercise 6.4, where you distinguished the prepositional phrase with *to* from the adverbial infinitive phrase. In the previous exercise you saw the infinitive phrase used as a nominal. In this exercise you will find all three kinds of phrases using *to*: prepositional phrases, nominal infinitives, and adverbial infinitives. One helpful way to distinguish the adverbial infinitive is by its underlying meaning: In nearly every case it answers the question *why;* and it can be expanded with *in order: I went home to study = I went home in order to study.* And of course the nominal infinitive occupies an NP slot in the sentence pattern.

   Underline each *to*-phrase in the following sentences and label each as pp (prepositional phrase), nom (nominal infinitive), or adv (adverbial infinitive). Your instructor may also ask you to diagram these sentences.

Example:

   We went <u>to the computer show</u> <u>to check out the new war games</u>.
                      pp   **adv**

1.   Did you remember to check the connection to the Ethernet port?

2.   My ambition is to win a scholarship to clown school.

3.   Fate tried to conceal him by naming him Smith. [Oliver Wendell Holmes]

4.   To get a decent job, a person needs to have some experience.

5. Janelle is trying hard to ignore the rude remarks that her coach makes to her.

6. Some people go to great lengths to hide their fears.

7. A man must take a lot of punishment to write a really funny book.
   [Ernest Hemingway]

8. The greatest thing in family life is to take a hint when a hint is intended.
   [Robert Frost]

9. It is almost impossible to provide a definitive answer to your question.

10. You should consult an accountant to figure out the best way to secure a refund.

NOMINAL CLAUSES

Clauses that occupy nominal slots have all the qualities of sentence patterns: a subject, a predicating verb, and any required slots following the verb, as well as optional elements. The only difference between these clauses and the sentences we have studied so far is that these are not independent clauses: They are part of another sentence. But, like sentences, they can also be classified according to their sentence patterns.

Nominal clauses are introduced by two kinds of words: **interrogatives** and **expletives**. In the mountain bike example, the clause is introduced by the interrogative *who*, which fills the subject slot in its own clause:

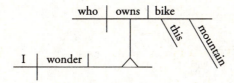

The interrogative always plays a role in the clause it introduces, but no matter what that role is, the interrogative introduces the clause:

I wonder <u>what brand this bike is</u>.

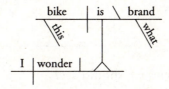

Nominal clauses are also introduced by the expletives *that, if, whether,* and *whether or not*. One important difference between the two kinds of introducers is that the expletive plays no part in its own clause, as the following diagram shows:

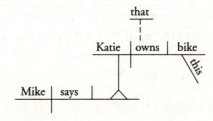

Exercise 8.5

Identifying and Diagramming Nominal Clauses

Directions: Each of the following sentences includes a clause in a nominal position. Underline the clause; identify its function in the sentence; then identify the pattern of the nominal clause. On separate paper, diagram the sentences in this exercise.

Example:

Do you know <u>where the children are?</u>

direct object—Pattern I

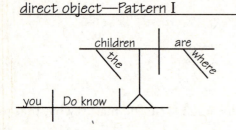

(Note that while this nominal clause is Pattern I, the main clause is Pattern VII.)

1. I forgot where I left my car keys.

    _____

2. Have you decided which movies we should see?

    _____

3. The best thing about the future is that it starts tomorrow.

    _____

4. His suspicion that someone was following him was a paranoid delusion.

    _____

5. I clearly remember I heard that song for the first time in Italy.

    _____

6. What the world needs is more love and less paperwork. [Pearl Bailey]

    _____

7. The students are wondering if the test will be easy.

   _____

8. She does not understand why you didn't call again.

   _____

9. What we call progress is the exchange of one nuisance for another. [Havelock Ellis]

   _____

10. How our team could have blown a twenty-point lead baffles me.

    _____

EMBEDDING

Like prepositional phrases, nominal clauses and verb phrases demonstrate the recursiveness of the language—the embedding of one nominal structure in another: nominal clauses, gerund phrases, and infinitive phrases can all be embedded in various ways. This kind of sentence building is a common and natural process, as the following exercise will illustrate.

Exercise 8.6

Identifying Embedded Nominals

A. *Directions:* On the line below each of the following sentences identify the form of the underlined embedded nominal—nominal clause, gerund phrase, infinitive phrase. Then name the function that the nominal performs within the structure in which it is embedded.

Example: I imagine that <u>commuting a hundred miles to work every day</u> becomes tiresome.

<u>gerund phrase; subject of nominal clause (of the verb "becomes")</u>

1. You never defeat danger by refusing <u>to face it</u>.

    _____

2. Knowing <u>that he was being followed</u> gave Roger the creeps.

    _____

3. When you don't know <u>where you are going</u>, any road will do.

    _____

4. My first mistake was forgetting <u>to peel the onions</u>.

    _____

5. If you have to ask <u>how much gas costs</u>, you can't afford it.

    _____

6. Believing in progress does not mean believing <u>that any progress has yet been made</u>. [Franz Kafka]

_____

B. *Directions:* Pick out all the embedded noun clauses, gerund phrases, and infinitive phrases in each of the following sentences; list them below the sentence and indicate the form and function of each.

Example: I told my nephew to stop asking our neighbor how old she is.

   to stop asking our neighbor how old she is—infinitive phrase, direct object of "told"

   asking our neighbor how old she is—gerund, direct object of "to stop"

   how old she is—clause, direct object of "asking"

1. Don't leave without telling your friends where you are going.

2. Attempting to finish my term paper after staying up all night was clearly a mistake.

3. We probably wouldn't worry about what people think of us if we knew how seldom they do.

Exercise 8.7
Identifying Dependent Clauses

Directions: You have studied three different kinds of dependent clauses—adverbial clauses, adjectival (or relative) clauses, and nominal clauses. The three are introduced by different kinds of words—adverbial clauses by subordinating conjunctions, adjectival clauses by relative pronouns and relative adverbs, and nominal clauses by expletives and interrogatives. And of course the three kinds of clauses function differently in their sentences: Adverbial clauses modify verbs; adjectival clauses modify nouns; and nominal clauses fill NP slots as subjects, direct objects, and so on. Underline the dependent clauses in the following sentences. Identify each as adverbial (adv), adjectival (adj), or nominal (nom); then give its specific function in the sentence. (If adverbial, what verb does it modify? If adjectival, what noun does it modify? If nominal, what NP slot does it fill?) Some clauses will be embedded within other clauses.

Example: Even before the fire alarm sounded, I sensed that something was happening.
               adv—mod. *sensed*   nom—dir obj

1.   How you spend your money is your own business.

2.   The tragedy of life is that people don't change. [Agatha Christie]

3.   He gave her a look that you could have poured on a waffle. [Ring Lardner]

4.   It is always the best policy to speak the truth, unless of course you are an exceptionally

     good liar. [Jerome K. Jerome]

5.   If you tell us your phobias, we will tell you what you are afraid of.

     [Robert Benchley]

6. The dying process begins the minute we are born but accelerates during dinner parties. [Carol Matthau]

7. Advice is what we ask for when we already know the answer but wish we didn't. [Erica Jong]

8. As the instructor came into the room, Duncan quickly threw a piece of canvas over the bust that he was sculpting.

9. A bore is a person who talks when you want him to listen. [Ambrose Bierce]

10. Conscience is the inner voice that warns us somebody may be looking. [H.L. Mencken]

11. A hundred and fifty years ago, when Hyman Lipman patented the world's first pencil with an attached eraser, he certainly didn't anticipate that it would compete one day with BlackBerrys and online crossword puzzles.

12. Some school teachers felt that pencils with erasers encouraged carelessness because students didn't have to get things right the first time.

Exercise 8.8

Nominals and Sentence Patterns

Directions: (1) In the parentheses identify the sentence pattern of the main clause; (2) underline any nominal clauses or nominal verb phrases; (3) on the line below the sentence name the function of each underlined clause or phrase and identify its sentence pattern.

Example: I hope <u>that the rain stops soon</u>. <u>(VII)</u>

<u>direct object—Pattern VI</u>

1. Deanna's career goal is to become a physical therapist. (_____)

   _____

2. After eating a big meal, I usually feel drowsy. (_____)

   _____

3. What Carlos said about his supervisor really surprised everybody. (_____)

   _____

4. The coach promised to throw the team a huge victory celebration. (_____)

   _____

5. The work crew decided to knock off for the day. (_____)

   _____

6. Sheri's mother says she wants to go back to college. (_____)

   _____

7. Millions of TV viewers are wondering which contestant will be voted off the show next week. (_____)

   _____

8. Dyeing your hair auburn was a bad idea. (_____)

   _____

9. Doctors insist that weight loss is the key to controlling Type 2 diabetes.
   (_____)

   _____

10. Insanity is doing the same thing over and over again but expecting different results.

    [Rita Mae Brown] (_____)

    _____

Using separate paper, diagram the ten sentences in this exercise. Remember that you have already done a great deal of the analysis for those diagrams: You have identified the sentence pattern of each main clause as well as both the sentence pattern and the function of each embedded clause and verb phrase. With that information you know what the skeletal diagram will look like.

Example:

I hope that the rain stops soon.

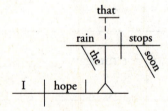

Exercise 8.9
Identifying Nominal Form and Function

Directions: The underlined elements in the following paragraph are nominal in function. On the lines following the passage identify, first, the *form* of each and, second, its *specific function*. *Form* includes such labels as noun, noun phrase, infinitive phrase, gerund phrase, and clause; *function* refers to the sentence slots—subject, direct object, object of preposition, etc. You'll find it helpful to picture the sentence on a diagram.

My son was always <u>an avid collector</u> in his youth. <u>Collecting stamps</u> was
                                    1   2

<u>his favorite hobby</u>. I suspect <u>that he's now tired of his youthful pastime</u>.
     3   4

<u>His biggest collection</u> in the old days, <u>stamps with pictures of African flora and fauna</u>,
    5   6

is now collecting dust in <u>our attic</u>. After <u>having it appraised by a stamp expert</u>, he says
                          7   8

he is planning <u>to sell it</u>. I wonder <u>if it's worth a lot</u>.
              9   10

Form	**Function**
1. _____	_____
2. _____	_____
3. _____	_____
4. _____	_____
5. _____	_____
6. _____	_____
7. _____	_____
8. _____	_____
9. _____	_____
10. _____	_____

Test Exercise 8.10

Identifying Form and Function

Directions: This exercise is similar to the previous one except that it is not confined only to nominals; it includes modifiers that you are familiar with. Identify each of the underlined elements according to both its form and its function. *Form* refers to word categories (noun, verb, preposition, etc.), names of phrases (prepositional phrase, noun phrase, gerund phrase, etc.), and clauses. *Function* refers to the specific role the word or word group plays in the sentence: subject, direct object, modifier of *run*, etc. Again, you'll find it helpful to picture the sentence on a diagram to figure out the function of the underlined item. [Answers are not given.]

Examples:	**Form**	**Function**
I think <u>that studying history is fascinating</u>.	nominal clause	dir obj
I think that <u>studying history</u> is fascinating.	gerund phrase	subject

1. My little brother enjoys <u>playing computer games</u>. _____ _____

2. <u>Winning computer</u> games gives him great satisfaction. _____ _____

3. Winning computer games gives him <u>great satisfaction</u>. _____ _____

4. What he does with his time is <u>his own business</u>. _____ _____

5. <u>What he does with his time</u> is his own business. _____ _____

6. Maria is planning <u>to go to law school in the fall</u>. _____ _____

7. <u>To get into a good law school</u> is not easy. _____ _____

8. Maria is planning to go to law school <u>in the fall</u>.   _____   _____

9. I think <u>that being a lawyer would be exciting</u>.   _____   _____

10. The elections on our campus <u>rarely</u> bring out many voters.   _____   _____

11. The elections on our campus rarely bring out <u>many voters</u>.   _____   _____

12. Many students obviously consider <u>the student elections</u> unimportant.   _____   _____

13. Many students obviously consider the student elections <u>unimportant</u>.   _____   _____

14. They do think <u>national elections are important</u>.   _____   _____

15. They do think <u>national elections</u> are important.   _____   _____

16. Our friend from Tampa spent last winter <u>with us</u> in Idaho.   _____   _____

17. He often wondered <u>if winter would ever end</u>.   _____   _____

18. <u>Worrying</u> gives a small thing a big shadow.   _____   _____

19. Worrying gives a small thing <u>a big shadow</u>.   _____   _____

20. Worrying gives <u>a small thing</u> a big shadow.   _____   _____

Chapter 9

Sentence Modifiers

As you learned in Chapter 9 of *Understanding English Grammar,* the term **sentence modifier** refers to any word or word group that modifies the sentence as a whole rather than a specific part of it. Many sentence modifiers are parenthetical. As **independent words and phrases,** they are nearly always set off by a comma when they appear at the opening or closing of the sentence and by two commas when they appear in the middle:

Luckily, I got a refund.

Rap music bores me, to tell the truth.

Shawn, on the other hand, loves it.

These parenthetical comments affect the pace of the sentence by slowing the reader down, by interrupting the main idea, or by shifting or focusing the reader's attention. The commas signal the reader that the word or phrase is an added comment, much like the nonrestrictive modifiers you saw in the discussion of adjectivals.

There are two other important classes of sentence modifiers. The **adverb clause** is connected to the main clause with a subordinating conjunction (such as *if, when, although, because*):

When I have time, I will return your call.

The **absolute phrase**—a noun headword with a postnoun modifier, usually a participle— adds a detail about the sentence as a whole:

His voice trembling, the valedictorian began his speech.

Exercise 9.1
Punctuating Sentence Modifiers

Directions: Add punctuation to the following sentences, if necessary.

1. As you may know our family likes to travel together in the summer.

2. On our trip out West we went to parts of the country that I had never seen before.

3. Much to my surprise the landscape was absolutely flat in eastern Montana.

4. I expected for some reason to see rolling hills there.

5. In western Montana on the other hand we were awed by the grandeur and beauty of the Rocky Mountains.

6. Glacier National Park for instance is simply stunning.

7. There was a terrific thunderstorm on our first night back home.

8. Luckily the storm did not cause a great deal of damage.

9. The power unfortunately was out for several hours.

10. By the way did you notice all the trashcans overturned on the sidewalk the next morning?

11. More wind and rain are on the way according to the latest weather report.

12. The weather in my opinion is getting more volatile every year.

Exercise 9.2

Using Subordinate Clauses

Directions: Turn the following complete sentences into subordinate clauses by (1) adding a subordinator in the opening position and (2) adding the resulting subordinate clause to another sentence as a modifier. You will have to supply the main clause. For a list of subordinating conjunctions, see page 73.

Example:

The party ended at midnight.

Because the party ended at midnight, we got home earlier than we had expected.

or

If the party ended at midnight, why didn't you get home before 3:00 a.m.?

1. The weather turned hot and muggy.

    _____

    _____

2. I hit the gas pedal instead of the brake.

    _____

    _____

3. There was an explosion in the building across the street.

    _____

    _____

4. The Merced River flooded Yosemite National Park.

    _____

    _____

5. Steroid use among professional athletes has been in the news again.

_____

_____

6. The laws about food labeling have not curbed the consumption of saturated fats.

_____

_____

7. Several parental groups are calling for legislative action to stop Internet bullying.

_____

_____

8. The state of Nevada gets most of its revenue from the gambling industry.

_____

_____

9. The number of family farms in the United States continues to shrink with each passing year.

_____

_____

10. Fran can't decide whether to buy a hybrid or a motorcycle.

_____

_____

ELLIPTICAL CLAUSES

An **elliptical clause** is a clause from which a word or words have been omitted, often the subject and part of the verb:

> While [he was] attending a play at Ford's Theater, President Lincoln was shot by John Wilkes Booth.

An elliptical clause will "dangle" when the omitted subject is different from the subject of the main clause:

> *Dangling:* When beginning a job search, the university placement office can provide valuable advice.

To eliminate the problem of dangling, you can revise the main clause to make its subject match the implied subject of the elliptical clause:

> When beginning a job search, a student can get valuable advice from the university placement office.

Another solution to the problem is to write out the clause completely:

> When a student is beginning a job search, the university placement office can provide valuable advice.

Other problems with elliptical clauses are discussed in Chapter 9 of *Understanding English Grammar*.

Exercise 9.3

Recognizing and Revising Elliptical Clauses

Directions: Underline the elliptical clauses; then rewrite the sentences to eliminate their problems.

Example:

> When studying for a test, the first step is to psych out the teacher.

> When you are studying for a test, the first step is to psych out the teacher.

1. Before painting a car, the area should be free of dust.

_____

_____

2. The employees are more suspicious of the arbitrator than the owner.

_____

_____

3. Although hoping for good weather, the picnic tomorrow may, in fact, be rained out.

_____

_____

4. Your application can't be approved until after checking your credit record.

_____

_____

5. If paid within ten days, you will receive a five percent discount.

_____

_____

6. More cars are built in Canada than Mexico.

_____

_____

7. While doing my laundry, someone sent me a text message.

_____

_____

8. Tsunamis are much more dangerous to seaside towns than ships on the open sea.

_____

_____

9. When attending a concert or lecture, cell phones and pagers should be turned off.

_____

_____

10. There was nothing to do while waiting for the rain to stop.

_____

_____

Exercise 9.4

Adding Absolute Phrases

Directions: Add an absolute phrase as a modifier to each sentence. Remember that an absolute phrase is a noun phrase in form—a noun headword with a postnoun modifier. The absolute will either focus on a detail of the whole or explain a cause or condition. It can either open or close the sentence.

Example:

The winning candidate moved to the center of the stage.

The winning candidate moved to the center of the stage, her hands clasped

triumphantly above her head.

1. The speaker droned on interminably.

   _____

   _____

2. Pat tried hard not to think about the needle in the nurse's hand.

   _____

   _____

3. The bear cubs rolled around in their cage.

   _____

   _____

4. The monkeys performed like trapeze artists for the children.

   _____

   _____

5. The desert looked beautiful in the moonlight.

   _____

   _____

6. The dessert looked sinfully delicious.

   _____

   _____

7. The losing candidate stood at the microphone to read a statement to the roomful of unhappy campaign workers.

   _____

   _____

8. Snoopy lounged on the roof of his doghouse.

   _____

   _____

9. The rain beat against the windshield.

   _____

   _____

10. The committee members began to argue among themselves.

   _____

   _____

Test Exercise 9.5
Identifying Form and Function

Directions: On the lines following each sentence, identify the underlined items according to both form and function. Remember that *form* refers to word categories (noun, verb, preposition, expletive, etc.), names of phrases (prepositional phrase, noun phrase, gerund phrase, infinitive phrase, participial phrase, etc.), and clauses (nominal clause, adverbial clause, relative clause, subordinate clause). *Function* refers to the specific role the word or word group plays in the sentence: subject, direct object, appositive, modifier of *play*, sentence modifier, etc. [Answers are not given.]

	Form	Function
1. Did you see that last play, <u>Cindy</u>?	_____	_____
2. <u>Clearly</u>, the wrong player was called for the foul.	_____	_____
3. The fans considered that call <u>a real blunder</u>.	_____	_____
4. The fans hoped <u>that the referee would change his mind</u>.	_____	_____
5. Getting a referee to admit a mistake is <u>impossible</u>.	_____	_____
6. <u>Getting a referee to admit a mistake</u> is impossible.	_____	_____
7. <u>Their voices shaking the rafters</u>, the fans made a real difference in that game.	_____	_____
8. If we had won the game, we might have won the <u>league</u> championship.	_____	_____
9. <u>If we had won that game</u>, we might have won the league championship.	_____	_____

10. <u>Ironically</u>, losing that game
    made the team want to play harder.

_____   _____

11. <u>Feeling cheated by the officials</u>,
    the fans pledged to redouble
    their support.

_____   _____

12. They threw a party after the game
    <u>to forget their disappointment</u>.

_____   _____

Chapter 10

Coordination

In the preceding chapters we have looked at various ways of expanding sentences by adding modifiers to nouns, to verbs, and to the sentence itself. In this chapter we will look at another kind of sentence expansion: **coordination**. To coordinate words, phrases, and clauses, we use three kinds of connectors:

1. Coordinating conjunctions: *and, or, but, yet, for*

2. Correlative conjunctions: *both-and, either-or, neither-nor, not only-but also.*

3. Conjunctive adverbs: *however, therefore, moreover, nevertheless, so, yet,* etc.

Understanding the various kinds of conjunctions will help you use compound elements effectively.

Exercise 10.1

Adding Coordinate Elements

Directions: Revise each of the following sentences by turning the underlined item into a compound, using the coordinating or correlative conjunction shown in parentheses.

Example:

The students <u>studied</u> until 3:00 A.M. (and)

The students studied and partied until 3:00 a.m.

1. The children played <u>on the porch</u> all afternoon. (and)

   _____

   _____

2. I will work on <u>my math assignment</u> tomorrow. (either-or)

_____

_____

3. Pam <u>changed the oil</u> before leaving for spring break. (and)

_____

_____

4. Our teacher looked <u>cheerful</u> in class this morning. (yet)

_____

_____

5. Our visitors this weekend were <u>unexpected</u>. (but)

_____

_____

6. I <u>can</u> go with you to the police station. (and)

_____

_____

7. John can speak <u>Spanish</u> like a native. (both-and)

_____

_____

8. Juan can speak <u>English</u> like a native. (not only-but also)

_____

_____

9. My roommates are <u>going to San Diego</u> for spring break. (either-or)

_____

_____

10. I've decided <u>that majoring in math was a mistake</u>. (and)

_____

_____

PARALLEL STRUCTURE

As you read in Chapter 10 of *Understanding English Grammar,* an important consideration for coordinate elements is that they be parallel. A sentence is parallel when all of the coordinate parts are of the same grammatical form. The conjunctions must join grammatical equivalents, such as pairs of noun phrases or verb phrases or adjectives:

Noun phrases:	The university plans to build <u>a new library</u> and <u>three residence halls</u>.
Verb phrases:	They will also <u>remodel the administration building</u> and <u>repair the tennis courts</u>.
Adverbs:	<u>Swiftly</u> yet <u>gracefully</u>, Michele skated across the ice.
Prepositional phrases:	The line stretches <u>down the hall</u> and <u>out the front door</u>.
Nominal clauses:	I don't care <u>who you are</u> or <u>what you want</u>.

If you followed the instructions in Exercise 10.1, your coordinate elements should have turned out to be parallel.

Unparallel parts occur most commonly with the **correlatives**, the two-part conjunctions like *either-or* and *neither-nor*.

*For Kim's birthday present, I'll <u>either</u> buy a CD <u>or</u> a video.

It's easy to see the problem: The word group following *either* is a verb phrase; the one following *or* is a noun phrase. It's easy to correct the problem too. Just shift one part of the correlative pair so that both introduce the same kind of phrase:

I'll buy <u>either</u> *a CD* <u>or</u> *a video.* [noun phrases]

I'll <u>either</u> *buy a CD* <u>or</u> *rent a video.* [verb phrases]

Exercise 10.2
Identifying Correlatives

Directions: Underline the correlative conjunctions in each sentence, and below the sentence identify the grammatical elements that are connected.

Examples: Elephants are found <u>both</u> in Africa <u>and</u> in Asia.
prepositional phrases
The African elephant is <u>neither</u> the largest <u>nor</u> the heaviest mammal in the world.
adjectives

1. Either you leave or I will call the police.

2.   I have neither the time nor the energy for your trivial complaints.

3. People both admire tigers as beautiful animals and fear them as man-eaters.

4. Many species of animals spend most of their time either eating or sleeping.

5. This position requires not only specialized knowledge but also the ability to handle people tactfully.

6. He was either ignorant of the policy or unaware of its relevance to his job description.

7. While in his nineties, Bertrand Russell spoke both vigorously and eloquently against the development of nuclear weapons.

8. Neither what you say nor how you say it will affect my judgment.

Exercise 10.3
Revising for Parallel Structure

Directions: Rewrite the following sentences, paying particular attention to the unparallel coordinate elements.

Example:

My uncle's doctor told him to quit smoking and that he should start to exercise regularly.

My uncle's doctor told him to quit smoking and to start exercising regularly.

1. The community will always value her contributions, admire her fortitude, and we wish the best for her.

   _____

   _____

2. You can take either the written examination or ask for a personal interview.

   _____

   _____

3. The drug company wants test subjects with allergies but who are not smokers.

   _____

   _____

4. She had a strong desire to study literature and for becoming a medical technician.

   _____

   _____

5. Both hearing the judge's tone of voice and the look on his face made me nervous.

   _____

   _____

6. What you do with your money and the way you spend your time are of no concern to me.

_____

_____

7. You can either leave the car in the driveway or it can go in the garage.

_____

_____

8. I heard on the news that the police have not only arrested a suspect in the robbery but he has confessed.

_____

_____

9. Progressive education aims to teach students to be open-minded, thinking with logic, know how to make wise choices, having self-discipline and self-control.

_____

_____

10. The final step involves making a ninety-degree kick turn and then start the pattern over from the beginning.

_____

_____

Exercise 10.4
Using Conjunctive Adverbs

Directions: Combine each pair of sentences into a compound sentence, using a conjunctive adverb in the second clause. Use a semicolon to connect the two clauses. Remember that the conjunctive adverb is movable; it need not introduce the clause. Among the common conjunctive adverbs are *however, therefore, moreover, nevertheless, so, thus, likewise, furthermore, consequently, yet,* and *in fact.*

Example:

Tires are no longer manufactured in Akron, Ohio.
The city still calls itself "The rubber capital of the world."

Rewrite: Tires are no longer manufactured in Akron, Ohio; nevertheless,

the city still calls itself "The rubber capital of the world."

1. Language and speaking are natural behaviors.
   Every normal human child learns to speak at least one native language.

   _____

   _____

2. Children pick up their native language easily.
   They begin to speak toward the end of the first year and develop steadily thereafter.

   _____

   _____

3. Most people think that babies do not start to talk until they say their first word.
   Long before they produce intelligible words they are learning a great deal about sounds.

   _____

   _____

4. The chairman of the Planning Commission refused to allow our citizens' committee to present our petition.
He ordered us to leave the meeting.

_____

_____

5. I have seen every episode of *Lost* at least twice.
I still can't follow the plot.

_____

_____

6. The school board recently announced a possible deficit.
The board is planning to spend over eighty thousand dollars on computers.

_____

_____

7. Joel pleaded with Megan for hours.
She left on the 5:10 p.m. train for Boston.

_____

_____

8. Two months later they were back together again.
They plan to marry in October.

_____

_____

9. He used the wrong nails to put up the drywall.
They popped right out when spring came.

_____

_____

10. His daughter told him to use special nails.
He hated to follow her advice.

_____

_____

PUNCTUATION OF COORDINATE ELEMENTS

One of the positive outcomes of understanding grammar—especially the grammar of coordination—is the understanding of punctuation that comes with it. As you learned in Chapter 10 of *Understanding English Grammar,* there is an important difference between the punctuation of a compound sentence and a compound element within the sentence. When *and* joins a compound within the sentence, we use no comma:

> The mayor claims that the streets are clean <u>and</u> that they are safe.

Between sentences, however, we do use a comma with *and* when we join complete sentences:

> She also claims that the crime rate is low, <u>and</u> the latest figures support her claim.

Another possibility for joining the compound sentence is the semicolon, which we frequently use when a conjunctive adverb joins the two sentences:

> Violent crimes have decreased by 15 percent; <u>however</u>, burglary and auto theft are still on the rise.

We should note two additional punctuation conventions regarding compounding within the sentence:

1. When *but* is the conjunction, a comma is often called for to denote the contrast, or disjunction:

> > The police have cracked down on crimes against people, <u>but</u> not on crimes against property.

2. In a series of three or more items, commas are called for between the parts:

> > Crimes against people include murder, rape, robbery, <u>and</u> aggravated assault.

(Some writers regularly omit that last comma, the one before the *and* in a series.)

Exercise 10.5
Punctuating Coordinate Structures

Directions: Add punctuation to the following sentences—if they need it.

1. I took piano lessons for several years as a child but I never did like to practice.

2. When I started college I surprised both my mother and my former piano teacher by signing up for lessons and now I practice every spare minute I can find.

3. My hands are small however I have exercised my fingers and now have managed to stretch an octave.

4. My fingers are terribly uncoordinated but every week the exercises and scales get easier to play.

5. I was really embarrassed the first few times I practiced on the old upright in our dorm lounge but now I don't mind the weird looks I get from people.

6. Some of my friends even hum along or tap their feet to help me keep time.

7. I have met three residents on my floor who are really good pianists they've been very helpful to me when I've asked them for advice.

8. When I'm in my room studying I often play my collection of Glenn Gould records for inspiration.

9. I'm so glad that Bach and Haydn and Schumann composed music simple enough for beginners.

10. I'm looking forward to seeing the look on my mother's face when I go home at the end of the term and play some of my lessons from *The Little Bach Book* she will be amazed.

Chapter 11

Words and Word Classes

In the three chapters of Part IV in *Understanding English Grammar*, you took a close look at how words are formed and classified. You learned about morphemes, form-class words, structure-class words, and pronouns. The exercises in this chapter will give you further practice in understanding the grammar of words.

INFLECTION AND DERIVATION

As you learned in Chapters 11 and 12 of *Understanding English Grammar*, words are made up of **bases** and **affixes**. The base gives a word its primary meaning. An affix attached at the beginning is a **prefix**; one attached to the end is a **suffix**. **Inflectional** suffixes express some kind of grammatical information—like plural or past tense—but do not change the basic category of a word. English has only eight inflectional suffixes. They help us to identify the category of a word. We know *talked* is a verb, for example, because it has the suffix *-ed*, an ending that gets attached only to verbs.

   Derivational affixes, on the other hand, usually change the class of a word. For example, *educate* is a verb, but the addition of *-ion* turns it into a noun—*education*. All prefixes are derivational, and any suffix that's not inflectional will be derivational. English has numerous derivational affixes. We can sometimes identify a word because it ends in a particular derivational suffix. For example, words ending in *-ion* and *-ment* (*instruction, accomplishment*, etc.) are nouns; words ending in *-able* or *-ible* (*lovable, flexible*, etc.) are adjectives.

   The first five exercises in this chapter will give you practice in using inflectional and derivational affixes to analyze and classify words.

Exercise 11.1
Derivational Suffixes

Directions: The words in the second column have been formed by adding a derivational suffix to those in the first column. Identify the class of the words in both columns: noun, verb, adjective, or adverb. Some words may belong to more than one class.

1. laugh   laughable
2. true   truly
3. day   daily
4. hand   handful
5. ideal   idealize
6. deep   deepen
7. real   realize
8. appear   appearance
9. gloom   gloomy
10. face   facial
11. press   pressure
12. wide   width
13. care   careless
14. edit   editor
15. lonely   loneliness
16. verify   verification

Exercise 11.2

Using Bases and Affixes

Directions: Each of the following groups contains a base and some affixes, both derivational and inflectional. Make a word out of each group. Name the class of the word you have made.

Example:

-s, -ment, place, re-   replacements—noun

1. -less, hope, -ly-   _____

2. -ed, short, -en   _____

3. -ize, -s, fertile, -er   _____

4. -ing, -ate, termin   _____

5. -y, -er, mess   _____

6. re-, -en, awake   _____

7. -dom, -s, king   _____

8. -s, -ist, violin   _____

9. -ate, -ive, act, re-, -ion   _____

10. dis-, -ity, able, -es   _____

11. -ly, -ion, -ate, affect   _____

12. be, -s, little   _____

13. province, -ism, -ial   _____

14. -able, stop, un-   _____

15. -ist, -ly, real, -ical   _____

16. -ion, im-, -able, press   _____

Exercise 11.3
Form Classes and Inflectional Endings

Directions: The following words belong to more than one form class. Write sentences that demonstrate two classes for each word. Underline the word and label its class.

Examples:

room

There are three <u>rooms</u> in our apartment.
noun

My cousin <u>rooms</u> with three other sophomores this year.
verb

warm

Our hands got too <u>warm</u> when we <u>warmed</u> them over the fire.
adj   verb

1. doubt

2. watch

3. cool

4. pitch

5. dry

6. dim

7. kind

8. break

9. light

10. fast

HOMONYMS

Homonyms are words that have the same sound and the same spelling but have different meanings: *saw* (the tool) and *saw* (the past-tense verb). This same concept applies to morphemes—to parts of words that sound the same but have different meanings. The purpose of this exercise is to help you distinguish between suffixes that look and sound alike.

Exercise 11.4

Homonymic Suffixes

A. *Directions:* The suffix *-ly* is added to many adjectives to form adverbs of manner, as in *silent, silently; formal, formally; careful, carefully.* But this adverbial suffix has a homonym: the *-ly* that's added to some nouns to make them adjectives—*love, lovely; scholar, scholarly; man, manly; month, monthly.* This adjectival *-ly* is also used with some adjectives to derive a variation of the adjective with a different meaning: *sick, sickly.* Identify the following words as adverb or adjective; some may be both. Use each in a sentence to illustrate your classification.

Example:

softly (<u>adverb</u>)   The music played softly in the background._____

1. purely (_____)   _____

2. yearly (_____)   _____

3. lonely (_____)   _____

4. deadly (_____)   _____

5. worldly (_____)   _____

B. *Directions:* The *-er* suffix can be inflectional or derivational. As an inflectional suffix, we add it to adjectives to make the comparative form: *bold, bolder; happy, happier; cool, cooler.* As a derivational suffix, we add it to verbs to form nouns: *sing, singer; ride, rider; preach, preacher.* Identify the following words as nouns or adjectives. Use each in a sentence to illustrate your classification.

Example:

louder (<u>adjective</u>)　　The music was louder than we expected. _____

1. younger (_____) _____

2. drier (_____) _____

3. loser (_____) _____

4. trucker (_____) _____

5. weaver (_____) _____

6. smarter (_____) _____

HOMOPHONES

A **homophone** is a word that sounds the same as another word but is different in spelling and meaning. For example, "new" and "knew" and "gnu" are homophones. In speech, you don't have to think about which one to select, but in writing you have to make a choice. And because the meanings are quite different, you really do have to use the right one or your readers will be confused. This exercise will challenge you to think closely about the meanings of sound-alike words—and to consult a dictionary when you're not sure.

Exercise 11.5

Choosing the Right Homophone

Directions: In the following sentences, fill the blanks with the words in parentheses to make a sensible statement; each word will fill one blank.

Examples: (sail, sale)   I bought a new <u>sail</u> for my boat at a clearance <u>sale</u> .
(weather, whether) Do you know <u>whether</u> or not the <u>weather</u> will continue to be mild this weekend?

1.   (read, reed). My cousin plays a _____ instrument in the orchestra but cannot _____ music.

2.   (discussed, disgust). As the consumers _____ the price of gas you could hear the _____ in their voices.

3.   (way, weigh) There is no _____ I'm going to _____ myself again.

4.   (mustard, mustered) He _____ all his courage and poured some of the extra-spicy _____ on his sandwich.

5.   (council, counsel) The city_____ decided to refer the matter to their legal _____ for an opinion.

6.   (bald, bawled) Tim almost _____when he looked in the mirror and saw how _____he was getting.

7.   (roomer, rumor) Have you heard the _____about the new _____ who moved in upstairs?

8. (bridal, bridle) The heiress did not _____ at the reporter's question about the male stripper at her _____shower.

9. (flocks, phlox) We planted _____ of pink and white _____ in our garden.

10. (muscles, mussels) Some bodybuilders eat _____, which are high in protein, to help develop strong _____ and tendons.

11. (earn, urn) She wants to _____enough money to buy a Grecian _____.

12. (all, awl) I'm sure _____ carpenters carry an_____ in their toolboxes.

13. (waive, wave) The librarian can _____ your overdue fines with a _____of the hand.

14. (tocsin, toxin) The American Medical Association has sounded the _____ about a possible _____ in bioengineered animals.

15. (naval, navel) There's no time to contemplate your _____in the middle of a _____ battle.

16. (beer, bier) Someone made the _____for this coffin out of wood from several old _____ kegs.

17. (knead, kneed) I asked the trainer to _____ the thigh muscles where an opponent had_____ me.

18. (pole, poll) The NCAA conducted a _____to determine which _____vaulter would represent the United States in the Olympics.

19. (ton, tun) That _____ of wine must weigh a _____.

20. (praise, prays, preys). I wouldn't _____ a con man just because he _____ for the victims he _____ on.

21. (chili, chilly) A bowl of hot _____ sure tastes good on a _____ day.

HETERONYMNS

Heteronyms are words that are spelled the same but differ in sound and meaning. For example, the noun *does*, plural for female deer, is pronounced to rhyme with *froze*; but the verb *does,* as in "He does not see us," rhymes with *was.* Similarly, *lead* is the name of a metal (rhyming with *bed*) and also the verb meaning "to guide" (rhyming with *feed*). The following exercise will give you practice in spotting and distinguishing between these tricky pairs of words.

Exercise 11.6

Identifying Heteronyms

Directions: Each of the following sentences contains a pair of heteronyms. Pick them out, identify their word class, and define them.

Example:

> The bass player had a bass painted on his t-shirt.
>
> bass (n.) = a musical instrument; bass (n.) = a fish

1. The nurse wound the bandage around the wound.

2. The garbage department cannot refuse to pick up a resident's refuse.

3. They shed a tear when they saw the big tear in their new couch.

4. The wind was so strong that we couldn't wind up the string on our kites.

5. The farmer fed the sow before going into the field to sow some wheat.

6. My Polish friend Sophia wears black nail polish.

Now see if you can write sentences to illustrate the difference between these pairs: *present* and *present; row* and *row; dove* and *dove; object* and *object; close* and *close.*

STRUCTURE-CLASS WORDS

In the previous exercises in this chapter, you identified and analyzed the components of **form-class words**—the nouns, verbs, adjectives, and adverbs that provide the lexical content in a sentence. In the following exercise you will be identifying and using **structure-class words**. These are the words that build grammatical structure rather than convey meaning.

The structure classes include *determiners, auxiliaries, qualifiers, prepositions, conjunctions, interrogatives, expletives,* and *particles.* They are called "structure-class words" because they supply the supporting structure for the form-class words. Unlike the form classes, the structure classes are relatively small and rarely add new members; and, with the exception of auxiliary verbs, they do not change form.

Exercise 11.7

Identifying Structure-Class Words

A. *Directions:* Label the class of each underlined word.

Example:

Trading stocks <u>on</u> the Internet <u>can</u> be <u>a</u> <u>very</u> risky venture.
          prep   aux   det qual

1. <u>The</u> passengers were detained <u>for</u> several hours, <u>but</u> they <u>were</u> finally allowed to board the plane just <u>before</u> it took off.

2. Miranda <u>was</u> being <u>rather</u> secretive about <u>her</u> new boyfriend.

3. <u>Our</u> survey team has <u>been</u> asking voters <u>about</u> their candidate preferences.

4. His cousin looked <u>on</u> in amazement <u>as</u> Ethan <u>very</u> carefully sprinkled cinnamon <u>and</u> bacon bits on top <u>of</u> his cereal.

5. She wears <u>her</u> morals as <u>a</u> loose garment. [Langston Hughes]

6. <u>There</u> were <u>several</u> old friends who showed <u>up</u> for <u>Dot's</u> debut performance.

7. <u>What</u> kinds of apples are <u>readily</u> available at <u>this</u> time of year?

8. The story is told <u>about</u> Winston Churchill that on <u>one</u> occasion <u>when</u> he <u>was</u> corrected for ending a sentence with a preposition he responded <u>with</u> something like, "This is the sort of nonsense up with which I <u>shall</u> not put."

B. *Directions:* Locate all the structure words in the following sentences; underline and label them as you did in Part A. The number in parentheses at the end of the item tells you how many structure words are in that sentence.

1. Any mother could perform the job of several air traffic controllers with ease. (6) [Lisa Alther]

2. The impersonal hand of the government can never replace the helping hand of a neighbor. (7) [Hubert Humphrey]

3. You can never be too rich or too thin. (4) [Wallis Warfield Simpson]

4. A résumé is a balance sheet without any liabilities. (4) [Robert Half]

5. The devil often cites Scripture for his purpose. (3) [Shakespeare]

6. In France cooking is a serious art form and a national sport. (4) [Julia Child]

Exercise 11.8
Recognizing Word Classifications

Directions: From each of the following sets of words, choose the one that does not belong in the same word class.

Example: would, may, should, want, will

want is a predicating verb; the others are auxiliaries

1.   after   at   with   upwards   into

2.   or   and   some   because   when

3.   college   class   instructor grammar   learn

4.   hungry   lovely   silly   obviously   angry

5.   provoke   must   insist   suggest   persuade

6.   an   my   all   how   first

7.   now   soon   friendly   badly   often

8.   very   quite   rather   many   too

9. happy   calm   peace   serene   joyous

10. built   garden   window   room   door

11. spinning   during   running   drinking   trying

12. belly   silly   bully   jelly   ally

PRONOUNS

Pronouns oil the wheels of good prose, helping avoid unnecessary repetition and moving a passage along smoothly. It's the writer's responsibility to make sure that each pronoun refers clearly to its **antecedent** (the noun it stands for). A pronoun with more than one possible antecedent can be puzzling. Pronouns can also be confusing if they do not refer to specific antecedents.

Exercise 11.9

Using Clear Pronouns

A. *Directions:* Examine the pronoun reference problems in the following passages. Then rewrite each passage to eliminate the problem. There may be more than one way to revise each passage.

Example:

> Clyde dropped his bowling ball on the patio and cracked it in three places.
>
> What does *it* refer to? The bowling ball or the patio?
>
> *Rewrites:* Clyde cracked his bowling ball in three places when he dropped it on
>
> the patio.
>
> Clyde broke the patio in three places when he dropped his bowling ball on it.

1. Marcie e-mailed her sister almost every day when she was on vacation.

   _____

   _____

2. Breathe in through your nose, hold it for a few seconds, and then breathe out through your mouth.

   _____

   _____

3. Several players arrived late for the team meeting, which annoyed the coach.

_____

_____

4. The employees learned last week that they are expected to enroll in an all-day business-writing seminar. This has caused considerable resentment.

_____

_____

5. Will told Sam that he needs to lower his expectations.

_____

_____

6. The police removed the wreckage from the scene and then photographed it.

_____

_____

B. *Directions:* On separate paper rewrite the following paragraph to get rid of all vague and ambiguous pronoun references. You may need to add words, take some out, or rearrange a few.

Myrtle and Marie were just finishing their second cup of coffee at Sandy's Country Kitchen when they told them they would have to leave. They complained that this wasn't fair, which they ignored. This made them furious, so she asked to speak to the manager, which proved to be a mistake. She came at once and told them that this wasn't a lounge; the restaurant was closing because they needed to go home. They protested that this was going to ruin its reputation for friendliness because they intended to tell all their friends about it. She said they could print it in the paper for all she cared, and then she turned on her heel and left them flabbergasted. Having no other recourse, they paid the bill and stomped out, vowing never to do it again.

Test Exercise 11.10

Identifying Word Classes

Directions: Identify the class of every word in the following sentences. Place your labels below the words: noun (n), verb (vb), adjective (adj), adverb (adv), determiner (det), auxiliary (aux), qualifier (qual), preposition (prep), conjunction (conj), expletive (exp), particle (part), pronoun (pro). [Answers are not given.]

Example:

A clean glove often hides a dirty hand. (English proverb)
det adj   n   adv   vb det adj   n

1. Money will buy a pretty dog, but it will not buy the wag of its tail. [Josh Billings]

2. Nothing happens until something moves. [Albert Einstein]

3. If love is the answer, could you rephrase the question? [Lily Tomlin]

4. Television has raised writing to a new low. [Sam Goldwyn]

5. Do not needlessly endanger your lives until I give you the signal.

   [Dwight D. Eisenhower]

6. You are young only once, but you can be immature forever.

   [Germaine Greer]

7. My folks did not come over on the *Mayflower*; they were there to meet the boat.

   [Will Rogers]

8. History teaches us that we have never learned anything from it.

    [Georg Wilhelm Hegel]

9. A lot of parents pack up their troubles and send them off to camp.

    [Raymond Duncan]

10. Show me a good loser, and I will show you a failure. [Paul Newman]

11. Now is the winter of our discontent / Made glorious summer by this son of York.

    [William Shakespeare]

12. She never lets ideas interrupt the easy flow of her conversation. [Jean Webster]

13. Nobody can be so amusingly arrogant as a young man who has just discovered

    an old idea and thinks it is his own. [Sydney Harris]

14. General notions are generally wrong. [Lady Mary Wortley Montague]

15. Success is a public affair; failure is a private funeral. [Rosalind Russell]

16. When the insects take over the world, we hope they will remember our picnics with
    gratitude. [Anonymous]

Chapter 12

Purposeful Punctuation

Chapter 16 of *Understanding English Grammar* summarizes the rules for using punctuation to mark boundaries, signal levels of importance, make connections, and add emphasis.

To make connections:

- Put a comma between independent clauses joined by a coordinating conjunction, but use a semicolon if the clauses already contain commas.

- Put a semicolon between independent clauses not joined by a coordinating conjunction.

- Put a semicolon between independent clauses when the second clause is introduced by a conjunctive adverb or adverb phrase.

- Put a colon between independent clauses if the second clause explains or amplifies the first one.

To signal levels of importance:

- Set off nonessential modifiers with commas.

- Set off interrupters with commas: transitional phrases, parenthetical comments, and nouns of direct address.

- Put a comma after introductory elements: prepositional phrases, one-word sentence modifiers, adverbial clauses and verb phrases, absolute phrases, and participial phrases.

To mark boundaries:

- Use commas to separate items in a series; use a semicolon if any of the items contain commas.

- Use a comma to separate coordinate modifiers of the same noun.

- Use a hyphen to join the elements of compound modifiers.

To add emphasis:

- Use a colon to introduce a list of appositives.

- Use dashes to highlight appositives, modifiers, and parts of compounds.

- Use parentheses to downplay explanatory or amplifying material.

The following exercises will give you practice in using punctuation for these purposes.

Exercise 12.1

Making Connections and Marking Boundaries

Directions: The punctuation marks and capital letters have been removed from the following passages. Rewrite them to make them readable again by adding punctuation marks and capital letters. Do not add any words.

1. The original version of this passage consisted of six independent clauses, marked by four capitals, four periods, two semicolons, five commas, one colon, one dash, and one hyphen.

    punctuation one is taught has a point to keep up law and order punctuation marks

    are the road signs placed along the highway of our communication to control speeds

    provide directions and prevent head on collisions a period has the unblinking final-

    ity of a red light the comma is a flashing yellow light that asks us to slow down and

    the semicolon is a stop sign that tells us to ease gradually to a halt before gradually

    starting up again by establishing the relations between words punctuation estab-

    lishes the relations between people using words

    —Pico Iyer, "In Praise of the Humble Comma"

2. The original version of this passage consisted of ten independent clauses, marked by five capitals, five periods, one comma, and five semicolons.

    i have grown fond of semicolons in recent years the semicolon tells you that there is

    still some question about the preceding full sentence something needs to be added

    it is almost always a greater pleasure to come across a semicolon than a period the

    period tells you that that is that if you didn't get all the meaning you wanted or

    expected anyway you got all the writer intended to parcel out and now you have to

    move along but with a semicolon there you get a pleasant little feeling of expectan-

    cy there is more to come read on it will get clearer

    —Lewis Thomas, "Notes on Punctuation"

Exercise 12.2
Signaling Levels of Importance and Adding Emphasis

A. *Directions:* Punctuate the following paragraphs to make them readable and rhetorically effective.

1. The original version of this passage included three commas, three dashes, and two hyphens.

    Most of the suspects were members of the Granger High School football team who had police said since June held up twenty two fast food restaurants and small retail stores. They were brazen police said they didn't even bother with masks. They were bold one or more allegedly carried a pistol to each crime. And they were braggarts as the robbery spree continued the boys apparently told their friends.
    —Mark Miller, *Newsweek*

2. The original version of this paragraph included two dashes, seven commas, and three hyphens.

    One of Buckminster Fuller's earliest inventions was a car shaped like a blimp. The car had three wheels two up front one in the back and a periscope instead of a rear window. Owing to its unusual design it could be maneuvered into a parking space nose first and could execute a hundred and eighty degree turn so tightly that it would end up practically where it had started facing the opposite direction. In Bridgeport Connecticut where the car was introduced in the summer of 1933 it caused such a sensation that gridlock followed and anxious drivers implored Fuller to keep it off the streets at rush hour.

    —Elizabeth Kolbert, *The New Yorker*

B. *Directions:* Examine the punctuation of the appositives in the following passage and answer the questions at the end.

Diane's mother, Phyllis, is a realtor. Her father, George, is a retired basketball coach.

Her cousin Mark also sells real estate, but her other cousin, Elissa, is still in high

school. Her sister, Lori, is a stay-at-home mom.

Why are the names *Phyllis* and *George* set off with commas? How many cousins does Diane have? How many sisters does she have? How do you know? Formulate a rule about the punctuation of appositives.

Exercise 12.3
Punctuating Sentences

Directions: Add commas, semicolons, colons, and dashes to the following sentences. Some sentences may not require any punctuation.

1. Before you complete your plans for vacationing at Lake Louise you should make plane reservations.

2. Reservations which may be made either by mail or online will be promptly acknowledged.

3. Reservations that are not secured by credit card or check will be returned.

4. Left-handed people can drive or sew or paint as well as any right-hander although it is not always easy for lefties to use many ordinary tools and mechanical gadgets.

5. Stores now sell objects designed especially for left-handed people watches scissors cameras and pencil sharpeners for example.

6. All students who can't swim must wear life jackets on the canoeing trip.

7. My cousin Melvin who can't swim has decided to stay home.

8. When TV is forced upon us all the things that give it power intimacy insularity intensity are deadened.

9. Severe unremitting pain is a ravaging force especially when a patient tries to conceal it.

10. While tulips are closely associated with the Netherlands the tulip in fact is not a native Dutch flower.

11. Like many other products in western Europe such as the potato and tobacco tulips came to Holland from another part of the world.

12. Most of the tulips probably originated in areas around the Black Sea in the Crimea and in the steppes to the north of the Caucasus.

13. Enchanted with tulips from the Middle East wealthy people in seventeenth-century Europe paid vast sums of money for one bulb in many cases the cost exceeded thousands of dollars.

14. Today three varieties of tulips are the most popular the Darwin which can be as large as a tennis ball and grows sixteen inches high the lily-flowered which has pointed petals and the parrot whose petals resemble feathers and which grows about seven inches high.

15. Robert Frost tells of a minister who turned his daughter his poetry-writing daughter out on the street to earn a living saying there should be no more books written.

16. Maria stepped up to the baseline positioned the racquet behind her shoulder tossed the ball into the air swung the racket forward with all her might and missed the ball completely.

17. Creativity is not the same thing as intellect in fact there is no relation between intelligence and originality.

18. Intelligence tests measure knowledge and skill but they do not accommodate inventiveness.

19. Creative people ask questions intelligent people want to know the answers.

20. The real interest rate the difference between the nominal rate and the rate of inflation has averaged about 3 or 4 percent over long periods.

21. Norwegian artist Jan Christensen placed his latest work *Relative Value* at a gallery in Oslo but it was quickly stolen and not surprisingly since the piece contained about $16,300 worth of Norwegian money stuck to it.

Answers to the Exercises

Answers are provided for odd-numbered items.

Exercise 1.1 (p. 2)

1. Ungrammatical. We're having pizza for dinner.

3. Grammatical. The standard, but awkward and affected form would be "For whom are you looking?

5. Ungrammatical. Eleven soccer players ran out onto the field.

7. Ungrammatical. Your three kittens are very tiny.

Exercise 1.2 (p. 3)

1. a truck (British)

3. a pharmacist (British)

5. a flashlight (British)

7. chips or potato chips (British)

9. an administrative or electoral division; a precinct (Canadian)

11. a line of people waiting to be served or to get in someplace (British)

13. a sofa (Canadian)

15. a cookie or cracker (British)

Exercise 1.4 (p.7)

1. Doesn't it look like the king? Or: It looks like the king, doesn't it?

3. Be true to yourself and you cannot, then, be false to anyone else.

5. Think not, you noble Roman, / That Brutus would ever go bound to Rome.

7. Why are you wearing your good clothes? Or: Why are you dressed up?

Exercise 1.5 (p. 9)

1. *To sail* originally referred to use of the wind; now it's used for any ship regardless of the means of propulsion.

3. *Starve* once meant to die in any manner; now it means to die from lack of food.

5. *Angel* originally meant a "messenger."

7. *Hussy* was once related to the word *housewife*; now it means "an immoral woman."

9. *Stupid* once meant "stunned" or "dazed."

11. *Alibi* started out as an adverb meaning "elsewhere."

Exercise 2.1 (p. 13)

A1. *stays:* verb—present tense, *-s* form; other forms would be *stayed, staying*
   time: noun—marked by determiner *a*; plural would be *times*, possessive would be *time's*

3. *waters:* noun—plural *-s* ending; marked by the determiner *the*
   abundant: adjective—can be qualified (*very abundant*); comparative and superlative forms would be *more abundant, most abundant*
   creatures: noun—plural *-s* ending; marked by the determiner *these*

5. *huge:* adjective—can be qualified (*very huge*); comparative and superlative forms would be *huger* and *hugest*
   sometimes: adverb—no form clues, but means "when" or "how often" and can be moved in the sentence

B1. The <u>new</u> <u>contestant</u> <u>appeared</u> <u>nervous</u>.
        adj   N   V   adj

3. Many <u>members</u> of the <u>crowd</u> <u>dutifully</u> <u>applauded</u> his <u>inane</u> <u>remarks</u>.
          N   N   adv   V   adj   N

5. The <u>astute</u> <u>critics</u> <u>panned</u> the <u>show</u> <u>mercilessly</u>.
      adj   N   V   N   adv

Exercise 2.2 (p. 17)

A1. ⟨My⟩ <u>relatives</u> have ⟨many⟩ odd <u>habits</u>.

3. ⟨Aunt Flo's⟩ umbrella <u>collection</u> decorates ⟨her⟩ front <u>porch</u>.

5. (My) older <u>brother</u> built (a) geodesic <u>dome</u> for (his second) <u>wife</u>.

7. (Their) maternal <u>grandmother</u> dresses (her three) small <u>dogs</u> in colorful <u>sweaters</u>.

9. (This) eccentric <u>behavior</u> rarely causes <u>problems</u> with (the neighbors).

B1.   <u>They</u>   <u>My relatives</u>

3.   <u>It</u>   <u>Aunt Flo's umbrella collection</u>

5.   <u>He</u>   <u>My older brother</u>

7.   <u>She</u>   <u>Their maternal grandmother</u>

9.   <u>It</u>   <u>This eccentric behavior</u>

Exercise 2.3 (p. 21)

1. to the top of the mountain [*adv*]; of the mountain [*adj*]

3. On a cold November afternoon [*adv*]; of Patagonia [*adj*]; at his public relations firm [*adv*]

5. from my study group [*adj*]; around the campus [*adj*]; on sunny days [*adv*]

7. in our botany class [*adj*]; about wild turkeys [*adj*]

9. with elimination rounds [*adj*]; on television [*adj*]

Exercise 3.1 (p. 27)

1. Tryouts for the spring musical | begin | in a few days. (VI)
    NP   V   prep phr
    subj   pred vb   adv

3. My girlfriend | is | extremely nervous | about her audition. (II)
    NP   V   qualified adj   prep phr
    subj   pred vb   subj comp   adv

5. Her parents | consider | that performance | a great theatrical triumph. (X)
    NP   V   NP   NP
    subj   pred vb   dir obj   obj comp

7. My roommate | remains | confident | of his chances. (IV)
    NP   V   adj   prep phr
    subj   pred vb   subj comp   adv

9. They | graciously | give | their fellow actors | a hearty round of applause. (VIII)
   Prn   adv   V   NP   NP
   subj   pred vb   ind obj   dir obj

Diagrams:

1.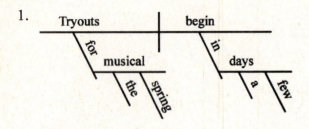

3.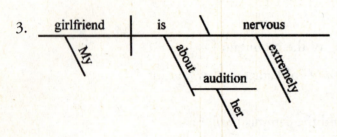

5.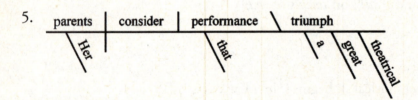

7.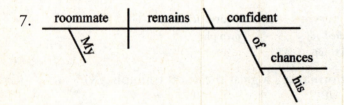

9.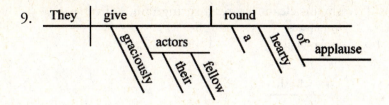

Exercise 3.2 (p. 30)

1. linking, pattern IV

3. linking, pattern V

5. transitive, pattern VII

7. transitive, pattern VII

9. transitive, pattern VII

11. linking, pattern IV

13. intransitive, pattern VI

15. linking, pattern IV

17. linking, pattern V

Exercise 3.3 (p. 31)
Answers with diagrams:

1. You | nearly | sideswiped | that squad car across the street. (VII)
   Prn   adv   V   NP
   subj   pred vb   dir obj

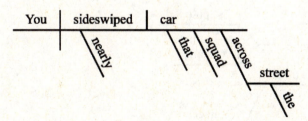

3. The air | always | seems | fresh and clean | after a spring rain. (IV)
    NP   adv   V   comp adjs   prep phr
    subj   pred vb   subj comp   adv

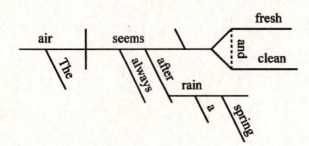

5. Thousands of families in the Midwest | still | live | in Sears houses. (VI)
    NP   adv   V   prep phr
    subj   pred vb   adv

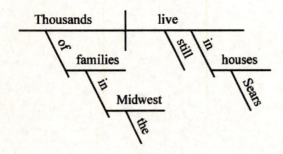

7. During rush hour | my new car | sputtered and stalled | in the middle of a busy
    prep phr   NP   compd vb   prep phr
    adv   subj   pred vb   adv

intersection.(VI)

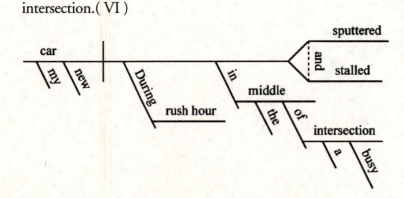

9. The exchange student from Naples | fixed | our soccer team | a traditional

                  NP   V   NP

                  subj   pred vb   ind obj

Scilian meal.(VIII)

         NP

        dir obj

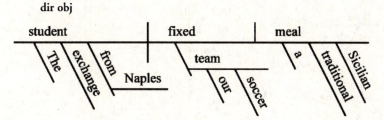

11. The candidate | made | her position on healthcare | very clear.(IX)

           NP   V   NP   qualified adj

           subj   pred vb   dir obj   obj comp

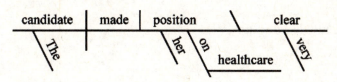

Exercise 3.4 (p. 34)

1. The ski lift | shut down | for the summer. (VI)

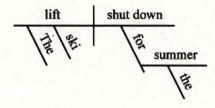

3. The fugitive | fled | down the alley. (VI)

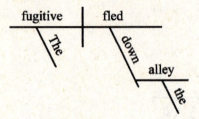

5. The defendant | stood by | her story. (VII)

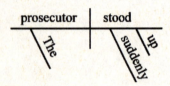

7. The prosecutor | suddenly | stood up (VI)

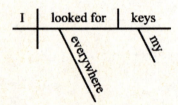

9. I | looked for | my keys | everywhere. (VII)

I | looked for | keys
everywhere
my

Exercise 3.5 (p. 35)

A1. declarative (VII)

3. imperative (VIII)

5. exclamatory (III)

7. declarative (VI)

9. imperative (IX)

Exercise 4.1 (p. 41)

1. has won: pres + have + -en + win

3. have been planning: pres + have + -en + be +-ing + plan

5. had expected: past + have + -en + expect

7. understand: pres + understand

9. can be: pres + can + be

Exercise 4.2 (p. 43)

1. were reading

3. were being

5. have been finishing

7. were going

9. had had

Exercise 4.3 (p. 46)

1. *Pleaded* is traditionally the preferred form, but *pled* is acceptable in American English.

3. *Sneaked* is considered standard, especially in formal written English, but widespread use of *snuck* has become common in speech; it is now used by educated speakers in all regions.

5. Regional American dialects vary in the use of these two verbs. Northern dialects seem to favor *woke; waked* is heard more often in Southern dialects, as in "The baby waked up early." However, both usages are considered acceptable.

7. *Dived* is the older from and is preferred by some, but both past tense forms are acceptable.

9. *Knit* is the predominant form; *knitted* is considered an acceptable variant.

Exercise 4.4 (p. 48)

Our cat loves to __sit (or lie)__ in the sun. Every morning after the sun __rises__, when I __raise__ the window shade, the cat jumps up and __sits (or lies)__ on the window sill. Our dog, however, is a lazy creature who would rather __lie__ around on the rug all day and sleep. Yesterday he __lay__ there the entire day. Once in a while he __raises__ his head from the rug and looks around to see what the cat is doing. Sometimes my mother takes the cat outdoors and __sets__ her on the porch swing. She __sits__ there for hours.

Exercise 5.1 (p. 53)

1. past + invent; past + be + -en + invent

   The indelible marker was invented by Sidney Rosenthal in 1952.

3. pres + have + -en + use; pres + have + -en + be + -en + use

   Magic Markers have been used for branding cattle, camouflaging fishing lines, and marking up buildings and subway cars.

5. pres + have + -en + alter; pres + have + -en + be + -en + alter

   Our vacation plans for the summer have been altered by [because of] the price of gasoline.

7. pres + will + regulate ; pres + will + be + -en + regulate

   The humidity in the nurseries will be regulated by the new air-conditioning unit.

9. past + can + have + -en + overlook; past + can + have + -en + be + -en + overlook

   Some important evidence could have been overlooked [by the prosecutor].

Exercise 5.2 (p. 57)

1. Someone turned in my wallet to the lost-and-found department. (VII)

3. More than 17,000 islands make up the country of Indonesia. (VII)

5. Raoul keeps his valuables in a safe in his office. (VII)

7. The bank approved Paula's credit card application. (VII)

9. Members of Congress are calling the president's economic plan a failure. (X)

Exercise 5.3 (p. 59)

1. (A) In the Middle Ages thousands of manuscripts were copied by hand by monks.

3. (P) The real estate agent leased the apartment to us under false pretenses.

5. (P) The Channel Tunnel has considerably reduced the travel times between London and Paris.

7. (P) People in three neighboring states could feel the earthquake.

9. (P) You should dice the fruit and soak it in brandy.

Exercise 5.5 (p. 63)

These are some possibilities; you may think of others.

A1.   It was the onions that ruined the stew.

   It was the stew that the onions ruined.

3.   It was Ruth's father who won $500 in an amateur photography contest.

   It was $500 that Ruth's father won in an amateur photography contest.

5.   It was Myrtle's special marinated mushrooms that added a gourmet touch to the salad.

   It was a gourmet touch that Myrtle's special marinated mushrooms added to the salad.

B1.   What I want is a good sleep.

3.   What hundreds of angry voters were protesting was the candidate's position on the war.

5.   What concerns a great many environmentalists is the encroachment of civilization on wilderness areas.

1. with art works by the French impressionists [*modifies* was filled];
   "by the French impressionists" is an adjectival prep phrase embedded in
   the adverbial.

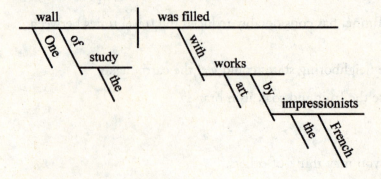

3. sometimes, from depression, during the dark days of winter [*all modify* suffer];
   "of winter" is an embedded adjectival prep phrase.

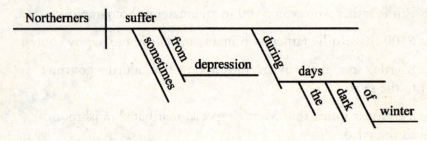

5. often, with good intentions [*both modify* is paved]

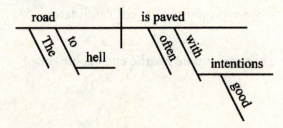

7. precariously, on the brink of extinction [*both modify* are teetering]; "of extinction" is an embedded adjectival prep phrase.

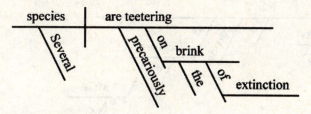

9. cautiously, into the dark alley [*both modify* crept]; quickly, against the wall [*both modify* flattened]

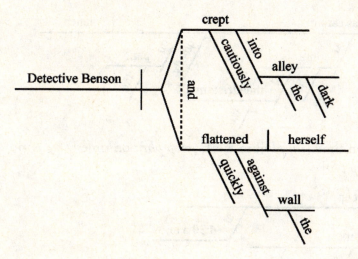

Exercise 6.2 (p. 71)

1. home [*noun*]; on Saturday [*prep phr*]; to prepare us a special dinner [*inf phr*]

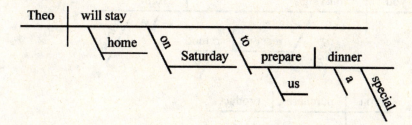

3. finally [*adv*]; this summer [*NP*]

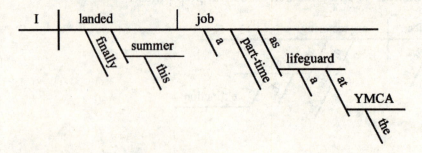

5. At the time of the thunderstorm [*prep phr*]; quietly [*adv*]; on the patio [*prep phr*]

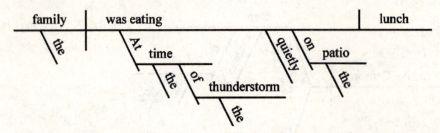

7. To get to work on time [*inf phr*]; to work [*prep phr*]; on time [*prep phr*]; at 4:30 a.m. [*prep phr*]

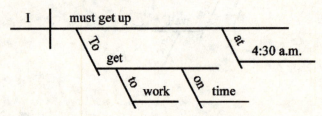

9. To receive a refund [*inf phr*]; before you purchase this product [*clause*]:

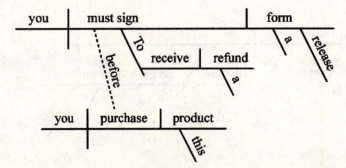

Exercise 6.4 (p. 75)

1. To keep its audiences happy [*inf—adv*]

3. to a college in Michigan[*prep—adv*]; to be near
   her family [*inf—adv*]

5. To get a better view [*inf—adv*]; to the top of the monument [*prep—adv*]

7. to get closer to the stage [*inf—adv*]; to the stage [*prep—adv*]

9. to the computer show [*prep—adv*]; to check out the new laptops
   [*inf—adv*]

Exercise 7.1 (p. 82)

1. In <u>my</u> opinion, <u>the candidate's</u> rash remarks have raised serious questions
      poss HW   poss NP   HW   HW
      pro

   for <u>many</u> voters.
      indef   HW
      pro

   [The possessive noun *candidate's* has its own determiner—*the,* an article.]

3. <u>Our</u> exams in <u>that</u> class would have challenged Luther Burbank.
    poss HW   dem HW   HW
    pro   pro

5. <u>Few</u> substitute teachers in <u>the</u> public schools can serve <u>a</u> full year without.
    ind   HW   art   HW   art   HW
    pro

   <u>any</u> problems.
    ind   HW
    pro

7. <u>Their</u> oldest son works in <u>his uncle's</u> office in Dublin.
    poss   HW   poss NP   HW   HW
    pro

   [The possessive noun *uncle's* has its own determiner—*his,* a possessive pronoun.]

9. <u>Our</u> team will probably win <u>the</u> division championship <u>this</u> year.
    poss HW   art   HW   dem HW
    pro   pro

Exercise 7.2 (p. 84)

1. in the United States [*adj*]; with highly paid soloists [*adj*]; because of financial difficulties [*adv*]

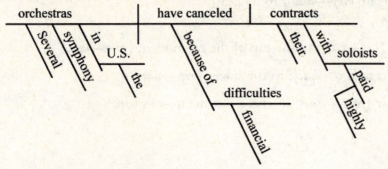

3. According to the National Institutes of Health [*adv*]; from carpal tunnel syndrome [*adv*]

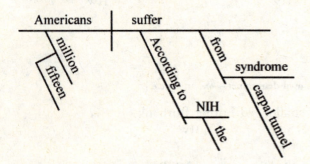

5. around the courthouse square[*adj*]

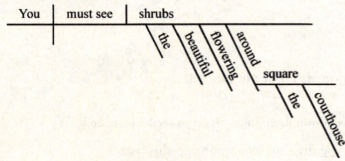

7. to the door [*adj*]; in the lock [*adv*]

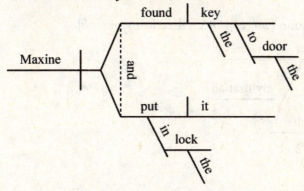

9. with the highest score[*adj*]; to Fiji[*adj*]

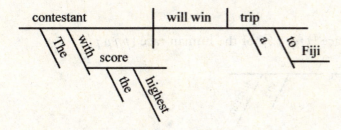

Exercise 7.3 (p. 87)

1. The familiar story <u>that Marco Polo brought pasta back from China</u> is just a legend. (*restrictive*)

3. The dried noodle-like product <u>the Arabs introduced to Sicily in the eighth century</u> is most likely the origin of dried pasta. (*restrictive*)

5. Italians traditionally cook their pasta *al dente*, <u>which is Italian for "to the tooth" and means "not too soft."</u> (*nonrestrictive*)

7. The many ingredients <u>that are added to pasta dough</u> include cheese, spices, and even squid ink. (*restrictive*).

9. Today pasta is more commonly made with special machines, such as extrusion tools <u>that force ingredients through holes in a copper plate.</u> (*restrictive*)

11. Dried pastas, <u>which often have ridges or bumps,</u> are designed to grab and hold sauces. (*nonrestrictive*).

13. Italians eat over sixty pounds of pasta per person, per year, easily beating Americans, <u>who eat about twenty pounds per person annually.</u> (*nonrestrictive*)

1. who hurled an insult instead of a stone [*adj cl*]; of civilization [*prep ph*]

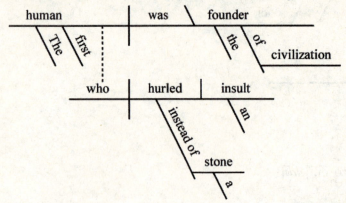

3. to the progress of the human race [*prep ph*]; of the human race [*prep ph*]

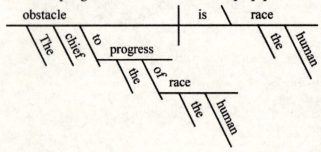

5. gazing at the stars [*part ph*]; at the mercy of the puddles in the road
   [*prep ph, functioning as an adj subj comp*]; of the puddles in the road [*prep ph*];
   in the road [*prep ph*]

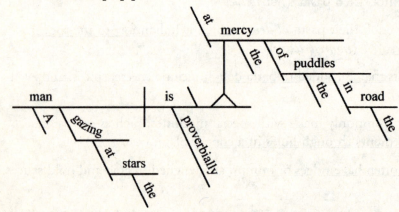

7. with the most stamina [*prep ph*]; to win [*inf*]

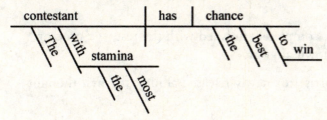

9. looking for an easier way to do things[*part ph*]; to do things [*inf*]

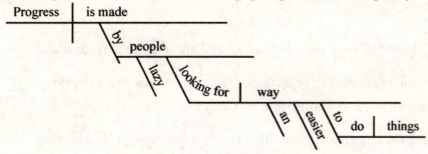

11. I dislike [*adj cl*]; of the vices [*prep ph*]; I admire [*adj cl*]

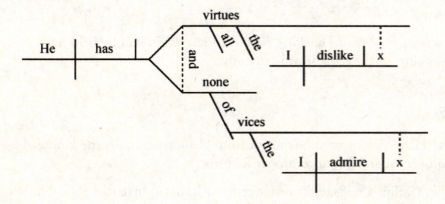

Exercise 7.7 (p. 97)

These are suggested revisions; you may come up with others.

1. Campaigning in 1960 as an exemplar of "vigor," John Kennedy was often forced to spend half the day in bed because of ill health.

3. To fix the problems with the draft of your essay, you need to go to the writing center.

5. Excited by the pounding music, we had no choice but to join the crowd on the dance floor.

7. Although the students were not completely finished with the test, the proctor told them to put their pencils down anyway.

9. When I heard about Alanis Morrisette's newly released album, my first thought was "Why?"

Exercise 7.8 (p. 99)

Good rewrites may vary.

1. In our neighborhood all dogs must be leashed and accompanied by an adult.

3. Abraham Lincoln wrote the Gettysburg Address on the back of an envelope while he was traveling from Washington to Gettysburg.

5. As I approached the coastal ridgeline, high cirrus clouds appeared, whipping across the moon like horsetails.

7. Few of us can forget our favorite teen movies, no matter how formulaic and sappy they were.

9. A memorial service for Maud Hawkins, who died last week, will be held next Wednesday evening, at the request of her family.

Exercise 8.2 (p. 105)

1. Representative Henry Waxman, a Democrat from California, chairs the House Committee on Oversight and Government Reform.

3. Richard Jordan Gatlin, a self-taught inventor from Indiana, invented the world's first successful machine gun.

5. Gatling, the son of a slaveholder, refused to sell his gun to the Confederacy.

7. Achebe's masterpiece, *Things Fall Apart*, is one of the first works of fiction to present village life from an African perspective.

9. You lack the one ability needed for this job—a commitment to the task at hand. [You could use a colon instead of the dash.]

1. winning the election in a landslide; to win the election in a landslide

3. losing her keys; to lose her keys

5. making too many mistakes on this biology homework; to make too many mistakes on this biology homework

7. giving the students an extra assignment; to give the students an extra assignment

Exercise 8.4 (p. 111)

1. to check the connection to the Ethernet port [*nom inf*]; to the Ethernet port [*pp*]

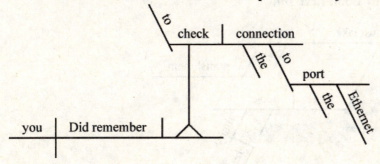

3. to conceal him by naming him Smith [*nom inf*]

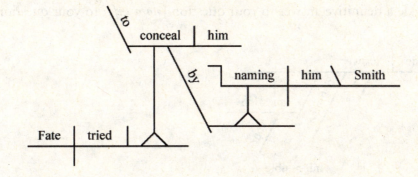

5. to ignore the rude remarks that her coach makes to her [*nom inf*]; to her [*pp*]

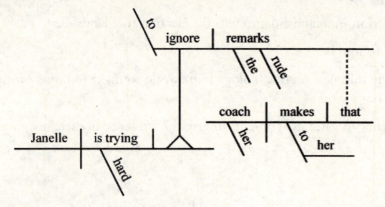

7. to write a really funny book [*adv inf*]

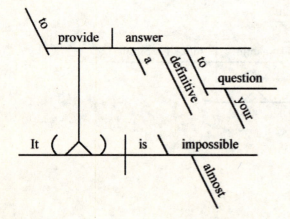

9. to provide a definitive answer to your question [*nom inf*]; to your question [*pp*]

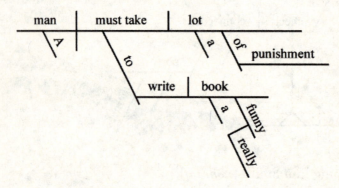

1. where I left my car keys [*dir obj*—VII]

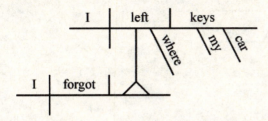

3. that it starts tomorrow [*subj comp*-VI]

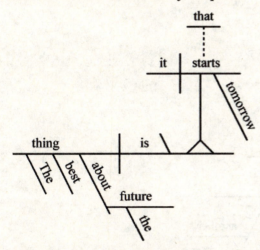

5. I heard that song for the first time in Italy [*dir obj*—VII]

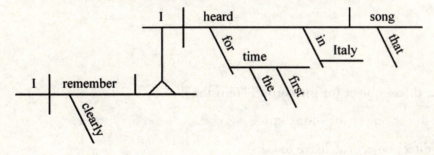

7. if the test will be easy [*dir obj*—II]

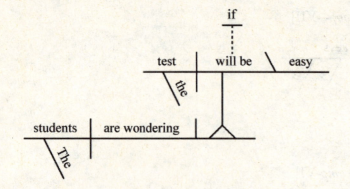

9. What we call progress [*subj*—X]

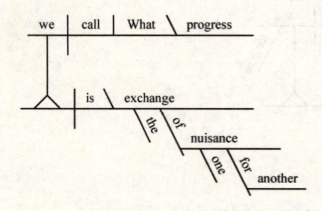

Exercise 8.6 (p. 117)

A

1. infinitive phrase; direct object (of the gerund "refusing")

3. nominal clause; direct object (of "don't know")

5. nominal clause; direct object (of "have to ask")

B

1. telling your friends where you are going —gerund phrase, object of the preposition "without"

where you are going—nominal clause, direct object of "telling"

3. what people think of us—nominal clause, object of the preposition "about"

   how seldom they do—nominal clause, direct object of "knew"

Exercise 8.7 (p. 119)

1. How you spend your money [*nom—subj*]

3. that you could have poured on a waffle [*adj—modifies* "look"]

5. If you tell us your phobias [*adv—modifies* "will tell"]; what you are afraid of [*nom—dir obj*]

7. what we ask for [*nom—subj comp*]; when we already know the answer but wish we didn't [*adv—modifies* "ask for"]

9. who talks when you want him to listen [*adj—modifies* "person"]; when you want him to listen [*adv—modifies* "talks"]

11. when Hyman Lipman patented the world's first pencil with an attached eraser [*adj—modifies* "didn't anticipate"]; that it would compete one day with BlackBerrys and online crossword puzzles [*nom—dir obj]*

Exercise 8.8 (p. 121)

1. (III) to become a physical therapist [*subj comp—*III]

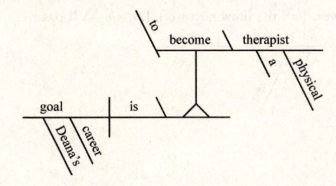

3. (VII) What Carlos said about his supervisor [*subj*—VII]

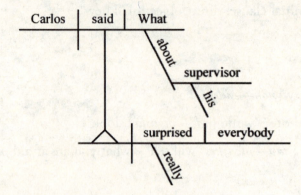

5. (VII) to knock off for the day [*dir obj*—VI]

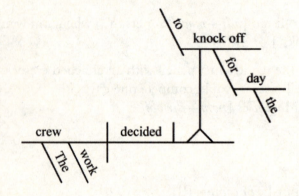

7. (VII) which contestant will be voted off the show next week [*dir obj*—VII passive]

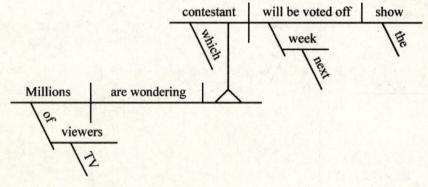

9. (VII) that weight loss is the key to controlling Type 2 diabetes [*dir obj*—III];
controlling Type 2 diabetes [*obj of prep*—VII]

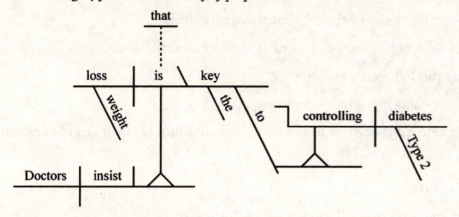

Exercise 8.9 (p. 123)

1. NP, subject complement

3. NP, subject complement

5. NP, subject

7. NP, object of a preposition

9. infinitive phrase, direct object

Exercise 9.1 (p. 128)

1. As you may know, our family likes to travel together in the summer.

3. Much to my surprise, the landscape was absolutely flat in eastern Montana.

5. In western Montana, on the other hand, we were awed by the grandeur and beauty
of the Rocky Mountains.

7. (no punctuation)

9. The power, unfortunately, was out for several hours.

11. More wind and rain are on the way, according to the latest weather report.

Exercise 9.3 (p. 131)

Some suggested rewrites:

1. Before painting a car, one should clear the area of dust.

3. Although we're hoping for good weather, the picnic tomorrow. . .

5. If you pay this bill within ten days. . .

7. While I was doing my laundry, someone. . .

9. When attending a concert or lecture, people should turn off their cell phones and pagers.

Exercise 10.2 (p. 140)

1. <u>Either</u> you leave <u>or</u> I will call the police.—*sentences*

3. People <u>both</u> admire tigers as beautiful animals <u>and</u> fear them as man-eaters.
   —*verb phrases*

5. This position requires <u>not only</u> specialized knowledge <u>but also</u> the ability to handle people tactfully.—*NPs*

7. While in his nineties, Bertrand Russell spoke <u>both</u> vigorously <u>and</u> eloquently against the development of nuclear weapons.—*adverbs*

Exercise 10.3 (p. 141)

These are suggested rewrites; you may come up with others.

1. The community will always value her contributions, admire her fortitude, and wish her the best.

3. The drug company wants test subjects who have allergies but are not smokers.

5. Both hearing the judge's tone of voice and seeing the look on his face made me nervous.

7. You can either leave the car in the driveway or put it in the garage.

9. Progressive education aims to teach students to be open-minded, think logically, make wise choices, and have self-discipline and self-control.

Exercise 10.5 (p. 146)

1. I took piano lessons for several years as a child, but I never did like to practice.

3. My hands are small; however, I have exercised my fingers and now have managed to stretch an octave.

5. I was really embarrassed the first few times I practiced on the old upright in our dorm lounge, but now I don't mind the weird looks I get from people.

7. I have met three residents on my floor who are really good pianists; they've been very helpful to me when I've asked them for advice.

9. (no punctuation needed)

Exercise 11.1 (p. 148)

1. laugh—v[n]   laughable—adj

3. day—n   daily—adj [adv]

5. ideal—n [adj]   idealize—v

7. real—adj   realize—v

9. gloom—n   gloomy—adj

11. press—v [n]   pressure—n

13. care—n [v]   careless—adj

15. lonely—adj   loneliness—n

Exercise 11.2 (p. 149)

1. hopelessly—adverb

3. fertilizers—noun

5. messier—adjective

7. kingdoms—noun

9. reactivation—noun

11. affectionately—adverb

13. provincialism—noun

15. realistically—adverb

Exercise 11.3 (p. 151)

The sentences are suggested illustrations.

1. [noun] I have my doubts. [verb] I never doubted you.

3. [verb] The breeze cools us off. [adjective] I prefer the cooler weather of autumn. [noun] Keep your cool. [adverb] Play it cool.

5. [verb] I dried my hands. [adjective] This has been the driest summer ever.

7. [noun] It takes all kinds of people. [adjective] You're very kind.

9. [verb] Please light a fire. [noun] Turn on the lights. [adjective] You should wear lighter clothes.

Exercise 11.4 (p. 153)

The sentences are suggested examples.

A1. [adverb]It happened purely by chance.

3. [adjective] He is a lonely person.

5. [adjective] They lost all their worldly goods.

B1. [adjective] My younger brother is a cop.

3. [noun] you are a big loser.

5. [noun] My uncle is an expert weaver.

Exercise 11.5 (p. 155)

1. a <u>reed</u> instrument, cannot <u>read</u> music

3. no <u>way</u>, to <u>weigh</u> myself

5. city <u>council</u>, legal <u>counsel</u>

7. heard the <u>rumor</u>, the new <u>roomer</u>

9. <u>flocks</u> of pink and white <u>phlox</u>

11. to <u>earn</u> enough money, a Grecian <u>urn</u>

13. can <u>waive</u> the fines, with a <u>wave</u> of the hand

15. contemplate your <u>navel</u>, a <u>naval</u> battle

17. to <u>knead</u> the muscles, had <u>kneed</u> me

19. <u>tun</u> of wine, must weigh a <u>ton</u>

21. bowl of hot <u>chili</u>, on a <u>chilly</u> day

Exercise 11.6 (p. 157)

1. wound (verb) = wrapped; wound (noun) = injury or cut

3. tear (noun) = drop of fluid from the eye; tear (noun) = rip, hole

5. sow (noun) = female pig; sow (verb) = to plant seed

Exercise 11.7 (p. 159)

A1. det, prep, conj, aux, conj

3. det, aux, prep

5. det, det

7. int, qual, det

B1. <u>Any</u> (det), <u>could</u> (aux), <u>the</u> (det), <u>of</u> (prep), <u>several</u> (det), <u>with</u> (prep)

3. <u>can</u> (aux), <u>too</u> (qual), <u>or</u> (conj), <u>too</u> (qual)

5. <u>The</u> (det), <u>for</u> (prep), <u>his</u> (det)

Exercise 11.8 (p. 161)

1. *upwards* is an adverb; the others are prepositions

3. *learn* is a verb; the others are nouns

5. *must* is a modal auxiliary; the others are predicating verbs

7. *friendly* is an adjective; the others are adverbs

9. *peace* is a noun; the others are adjectives

11. *during* is a preposition; the others are present participles

Exercise 11.9A (p. 163)

Good answers may vary.

1. When Marcie was on vacation, she e-mailed her sister every day.
   When Marcie's sister was on vacation, Marcie e-mailed her every day.

3. The coach was annoyed when several players arrived late for the team meeting.
   Several players annoyed the coach by arriving late for the team meeting.

5. Will told Sam, "I need to lower my expectations."
   Will told Sam, "You need to lower your expectations."
   Will recommended that Sam lower his expectations.

Exercise 11.9B (p. 164)

Here is an acceptable rewrite of the first three sentences, with the changes underlined. Your revisions may vary.

Myrtle and Marie were just finishing their second cup of coffee at the Kozy Kitchen, when <u>a waitress</u> told them they would have to leave. <u>The surprised customers</u> complained that <u>they were not being treated fairly</u>, but <u>the waitress</u> ignored them. This <u>failure to respond</u> made them furious, so <u>Myrtle</u> asked to speak to the manager, <u>a request that</u> proved to be a mistake.

Exercise 12.1 (p. 168)

1. Here is the way the original was punctuated:

Punctuation, one is taught, has a point: to keep up law and order. Punctuation marks are the road signs placed along the highway of our communication—to control speeds, provide directions, and prevent head-on collisions. A period has the unblinking finality of a red light; the comma is a flashing yellow light that asks us to slow down; and the semicolon is a stop sign that tells us to ease gradually to a halt before gradually starting up again. By establishing the relations between words, punctuation establishes the relations between people using words.

Exercise 12.2 (p. 169)

A1. Here is the original version:

Most of the suspects were members of the Granger High School football team who had, police said, since June held up twenty-two fast-food restaurants and small retail stores. They were brazen—police said they didn't even bother with masks. They were bold—one or more allegedly carried a pistol to each crime. And they were braggarts—as the robbery spree continued, the boys apparently told their friends.

1. Before you complete your plans for vacationing at Lake Louise, you should make your plane reservations.

3. (no punctuation)

5. Stores now sell objects designed especially for left-handed people: watches, scissors, cameras, and pencil sharpeners, for example.

7. My cousin Melvin, who can't swim, has decided to stay home. [If the writer has only one cousin, then a comma would be placed after "cousin."]

9. Severe, unremetting pain is a ravaging force, especially when a patient tries to conceal it.

11. Like many other products in western Europe, such as the potato and tobacco, tulips came to Holland from another part of the world.

13. Enchanted with tulips from the Middle East, wealthy people in seventeenth-century Europe paid vast sums of money for one bulb; in many cases the cost exceeded thousands of dollars.

15. Robert Frost tells of a minister who turned his daughter, his poetry-writing daughter, out on the street to earn a living, saying there should be no more books written. [The appositive "his poetry-writing daughter" could be set off with dashes instead of commas—for more emphasis.]

17. Creativity is not the same thing as intellect; in fact, there is no relation between intelligence and originality.

19. Creative people ask questions; intelligent people want to know the answers.

21. Norwegian artist Jan Christensen placed his latest work, *Relative Value*, at a gallery in Oslo, but it was quickly stolen—and not surprisingly, since the piece contained about $16,300 worth of Norwegian money stuck to it.